In everything I do,

may my life always bring

Pleasure to you.

To Laura

Rick Muchow is a longtime friend of Mosaic [church], not to mention one of my favorite people. He is real, optimistic, insightful, and deeply committed to God and to people. It makes sense for him to write a book about worship. Worship is his heart and his gift to the church.
—ERWIN RAPHAEL McMANUS, AUTHOR
AND LEAD PASTOR OF MOSAIC

For many years Rick has helped create an environment where I've been ushered into God's presence through song. I'm thrilled that his insights are now available to help others do the same.
—DOUG FIELDS, PASTOR TO STUDENTS AT SADDLEBACK

A much-needed and timely book! Rick has spent a lot of time and thorough research with this important teaching tool. I pray it will reach and teach worshipers in many nations for generations to come.
—MORRIS CHAPMAN, RECORDING ARTIST, WORSHIP LEADER

I know the sincerity, conviction, and discernment of the man behind the answers of this book. It is because of this he is a hero of mine, and more importantly, my friend . . . Rick Muchow.
—DOYLE DYKES, GUITARIST

Published by J. Countryman®, a division of Thomas Nelson, Inc., Nashville, Tennessee 37214.

Unless otherwise indicated, all scriptures in this book are from *The New International Version of the Bible* (NIV) © 1984 by the International Bible Society. Used by permission of Zondervan Bible Publishers; *The New King James Version* (NKJV) of the Bible, ©1979, 1980, 1982, 1992, Thomas Nelson, Inc., Publisher. Used by permission; *New Century Version*® (NCV). Copyright © 1987, 1988, 1991 by Thomas Nelson, Inc. All rights reserved; *The New American Standard Bible* (NASB) © 1960, 1962, 1963, 1971, 1972, 1973, 1975, and 1977 by the Lockman Foundation. Used by permission; *The Holy Bible, New Living Translation* (NLT) © 1996. Used by permission of Tyndale House Publishers, Inc., Wheaton, Ill. All rights reserved; *The Living Bible* (TLB) ©1971 by Tyndale House Publishers, Wheaton, IL. Used by permission; *The Message* (MSG) © 1993. Used by permission of NavPress Publishing Group; *The Jerusalem Bible* (TJB) © 1968 by Darton, Ongman, & Todd, Ltd., and Doubleday & Co., Inc.; *The Good News Bible: The Bible in Today's English Version* (TEV) © 1976 by the American Bible Society; *The Contemporary English Version* (CEV), © 1991 by the American Bible Society. Used by permission; *The Holy Bible, English Standard Version* (ESV), © 2001 by Crossway Bibles, a division of Good News Publishers; *The King James Version* of the Bible (KJV).

All songs copyright © Rick Muchow unless noted otherwise.

J. Countryman® is a trademark of Thomas Nelson.

www.thomasnelson.com | www.jcountryman.com

Design by Kirk DouPonce, DogEaredDesign.com

Project editor: Kathy Baker

ISBN 1–4041–0355–4

Printed and bound in the United States of America

RICK MUCHOW

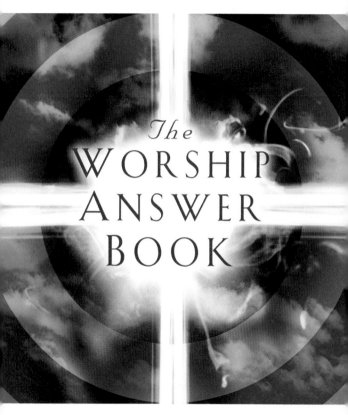

The WORSHIP ANSWER BOOK

MORE THAN A MUSIC EXPERIENCE

NASHVILLE, TENNESSEE

From the rising of the sun to the place where it sets,

the name of the LORD is to be praised.

—PSALM 113:3

FOREWORD

WORSHIP IS THE FIRST PURPOSE of your life. When Jesus was asked, "What is the greatest commandment?" he replied, "Love the Lord your God with all your heart and mind and soul and strength."

Rick Muchow and I have served God together at Saddleback for many years, and in our ministry we've operated from a simple definition of worship, based on the Great Commandment: *"Worship is any expression of our love to God—for who he is, what he has said, and what he's doing."*

When you understand worship in this way—in its full biblical context—then you can quickly see that there are many appropriate ways to express our love to God. Obeying, trusting, testifying, listening, praying, creating, thanking, waiting, singing, confessing, committing,

giving, and practically every other action can be an act of worship when our motivation is to demonstrate our love to God.

Although Rick is a gifted singer, songwriter, and musician, he is a joyful, living reminder that worship is more than music. In fact, worship is more than one part of your life; worship *is* your life. Rick is a worshiper of God, and he leads us to worship God. When he worships he models for our congregation and we follow his lead. Worship leadership is all about modeling worship for others. When people see Rick worship, it helps them think, *"I want that, too!"*

Of course, worship is not limited to songs we sing or even a worship service. The Bible teaches us to worship God continually and to praise him from sunrise to sunset (PSALM 113:3). We're to worship God at work, at home, in battle, in jail, and even in bed!

Worship should be our first activity when we open our eyes in the morning and our last activity when we close our eyes at night. The Bible says, "So whether you eat or drink or whatever you do, do it all for the glory of God" (1 CORINTHIANS 10:31).

How is it possible to do everything to the glory of God? By doing everything as if you were doing it *for* God. In worship, we turn our attention away from ourselves and toward God. When this happens, what we're doing becomes an act of worship that brings pleasure to God. My prayer is that God will use this book to help you live a life in constant worship of your Creator.

Worship of our Creator should become to us as natural as eating or breathing. In fact, God created us with a natural desire to worship something, and if we fail to worship God, we inevitably will find a sinful substitute. Everybody worships something. If not God, then we create an idol of something or someone or some task.

A lifestyle of worship also moves us beyond the halfhearted and hypocritical worship that is described in Isaiah 29. The prophet says people were offering God stale prayers, insincere praise, empty words, and man–made rituals without even thinking about what any of it meant. God says of such worship, "These people come near to me with their mouth and honor me with their lips, but their hearts are far from me. Their worship of me is made up only of rules taught by men" (ISAIAH 29:13).

Instead, God wants worship that bubbles from a heart of love, full of passion and commitment for him. For that reason, I've always believed there is an intimate connection between worship and evangelism. The goal of evangelism is to produce worshipers of God, and worship provides the motivation for evangelism. It produces a desire in us to tell others about Christ. The result of Isaiah's powerful worship experience (ISAIAH 6:1–8) was his request: "Here am I, send me!"

In genuine worship God's presence is felt, God's pardon is offered, God's purposes are revealed, and God's power is displayed. When nonbelievers watch believers relate to God in an intelligent, sincere manner it creates a desire to know God, too.

This is why I am so thrilled for this book to be released. One of the greatest blessings of my life has been to have my dear friend Rick Muchow as my partner in leading worship at Saddleback Church. Since he began serving with me years ago, we've watched our worship services grow from two to twenty–two per week and our attendance grow from one thousand to forty–five thousand on Easter at our twenty–fifth anniversary in 2005.

I have never met or even seen anyone on this planet who worships God with a more contagious joy and genuine humility than Rick Muchow. He is a living example of what it means to be filled with passion and gratitude for Jesus. His enthusiasm and authenticity continually push me toward deeper intimacy with God.

My prayer is that God will use this book as an instrument that pushes you to fully embrace the truth that God wants an intimate and loving relationship with you (EXODUS 34:14). May you love God with all your heart, mind, soul, and strength as you live according to his purposes!

— RICK WARREN
Senior Pastor, Saddleback Church
Author, *The Purpose Driven Life*

RICK MUCHOW IS A FRIEND of God. His personal walk with the Lord, forged through the fires of pain, loss, and sorrow, is strong. He has found God to be a refuge in times of trouble, and the Source of the joy that explodes when he leads us in worship. I can't begin to count the number of times I have come into a worship service feeling depressed or discouraged, only to start smiling as I watch my friend worship—his joy is contagious, and the way he blesses God leads me out of my despair into a place of renewed hope in God. His expressions of trust and confidence in the goodness of God inspire me to trust God as well. Rick has the ability to call out the best others have to offer—whether they be a musician, a singer, or part of the technical team. Choirs of men and women exuberantly sing their hearts out, responding to the passion he displays as he leads them.

He's not only God's friend, he's ours, too. I sure hope my mansion in heaven is near his so I can finally learn to dance like him!

–KAY WARREN

Introduction

THERE'S ALWAYS MORE to learn about worship. Even after being a worship leader for over thirty years, God used the writing of this book to ignite a fresh flame and intense hunger in my spirit for pursuing the wonders of God! King David of ancient Israel wrote, "One thing I have desired of the Lord, that I will seek: that I may dwell in the house of the Lord all the days of my life, **to behold the beauty of the Lord,** and **to inquire in His temple**" (Psalm 27:4 nkjv, emphasis added). Even as I write this, I am filled with a sense of awe and wonder about the incredible honor we have to worship God.

The questions in *The Worship Answer Book* came from believers and church leaders, family and friends—people from all over the world who've asked me about various worship issues. The truth is that what I think isn't that important; rather, the Bible is the best resource for understanding worship, and the answers in this book are drawn from the Word of God.

If you systematically look through the Bible for a doctrine of worship, a four-part foundation emerges:

- Biblical worship must be done in love. No love— no worship (1 CORINTHIANS 13).
- Biblical worship is always accompanied by humility and reverent fear (ISAIAH 66:2).
- Biblical worship is commanded by God (LUKE 10:27).
- Biblical worship involves surrendering your entire life as an offering to God (ROMANS 12:1).

The importance of understanding biblical worship— what God says worship is and how we are to worship him—can be seen in the so-called "worship wars" waged throughout the Church, not only in contemporary times, but also across biblical history. It could be said that the first argument over worship began with Cain and Abel when the issues of obedience to God and the motivation of the heart divided the two brothers (Genesis 4).

However, many of the arguments over worship today deal with methodology, not theology. It is absolutely critical that our theology regarding worship remain rooted in the Bible, which is the holy, inerrant, unchanging Word of God. On the other hand, methodology must change as the culture changes. The Bible allows for Spirit-led liberty when it comes to the methods we use to worship, but it insists on a theology anchored deeply in God's Word. There is no such thing as a style of theology; theology is either biblical or it's wrong.

When we encounter conflicts over worship style or methods, biblical theology suggests we pray and that we love each other dearly. James teaches us that we won't get anything by fighting or arguing. Instead, we should check the motives of our hearts and pray (James 4:2).

Having said all that, please hear me on this: *The Worship Answer Book* is not intended to provide ammunition for a battle about how someone else should or should not worship. Instead, it's designed as a tool to stimulate personal discovery and to help you consistently move into the presence of God.

While writing this book, I ran a quick Internet search on several words, including "worship." Here's a (nonscientific) breakdown for the number of webpages per topic:

- Books   793,000,000
- Music   616,000,000
- Money   358,000,000
- Sports   459,000,000
- Travel   519,000,000
- Worship   21,500,000

There were five hundred million more Internet links related to travel than there were for worship. Books, music, money, sports—all these ranked higher than worship by hundreds of millions of pages.

My point in mentioning this search is that the Church faces the intense influence of the world on matters of faith and worship. In addition, our own sin can also hold an unhealthy influence over our intimacy with God. For example, before I became a believer, music was my god and the guitar was my refuge.

Now, music is just one method I'm able to use to worship my Creator.

"Search me, O God, and know my heart."
—Psalm 139:23

From the early days of our faith, believers have acknowledged the God–shaped hole in each of our hearts. We constantly try to fill the hole because, with it empty, we feel that emptiness. In a simple sense, it is this hole that creates in us the desire to seek God and to worship him—because he is the only thing that can fill the hole. The God–shaped hole can only be filled by God's shape.

My prayer is that when God searches your heart, he will rank at the top of your list—ahead of books, music, money, sports, sex, or any other false god you may worship. (If not, he is faithful to forgive, and he invites you back to intimacy with him.) May God use this book to encourage you and those around you to become the kind of worshipers the Father seeks (John 4:23). Please use it as a study reference for your family, small group, worship team, or anyone with questions about worship.

> "O come, let us sing unto the LORD: let us make a joyful noise to the rock of our salvation. Let us come before his presence with thanksgiving, and make a joyful noise unto him with psalms. For the LORD is a great God, and a great King above all gods. In his hand are the deep places of the earth: the strength of the hills is his also. The sea is his, and he made it, and his hands formed the dry land. O come, let us worship and bow down: let us kneel before the LORD our maker."
> —PSALM 95:1–6 KJV

— RICK MUCHOW
Saddleback Church
Lake Forest, California

The
BASICS OF
WORSHIP

Worship has been stuffed in a small box for so long that it's difficult for many people to think of it as anything other than music or a church service on the weekend. Before we dig into the 'how' of worship, let's explore the basics of who, what, where and when we're to worship.

Happy are the people who live at your Temple;

they are always praising you.

PSALM 84:4, NCV

WHO DO CHRISTIANS WORSHIP?

Followers of the other great monotheistic religions—Judaism and Islam—sometimes criticize the Christian doctrine of the Trinity, saying we worship three gods. Even some Christians are confused about whether it is appropriate to worship Jesus and the Holy Spirit.

Christians worship the God of the Bible—and him alone. Jesus was very clear when he quoted from the Ten Commandments: "Thou shalt worship the Lord thy God, and him only shalt thou serve" (LUKE 4:8 KJV). Paul told the church at Corinth: "There is but one God, the Father, from whom all things came and for whom we live; and there is but one Lord, Jesus Christ, through whom all things came and through whom we live" (1 CORINTHIANS 8:6).

We need to be very clear about three things:

First, the Bible teaches that there is only one true God. "There is only one God" (ISAIAH 44:6 NJB). "Have we not all one Father? Did not one God create us?" (MALACHI 2:10). "One God and Father of all, who is

over all and through all and in all" (EPHESIANS 4:6).
"For there is one God and one mediator between God
and men, the man Christ Jesus" (1 TIMOTHY 2:5).
"You believe that there is one God. Good! Even the
demons believe that—and shudder" (JAMES 2:19).

Furthermore, the Bible uses many names for God.
Each name leads to a better understanding of the
nature and persons of God. For example, the Old
Testament name *Elohim*—a plural word that reflects the
fullness and completeness of God and hints at the
future revelation of the Trinity—describes God as
"God of all the earth" (ISAIAH 54:5), "God of all flesh"
(JEREMIAH 32:27), "God of Heaven" (NEHEMIAH 2:4),
"God of gods and Lord of lords" (DEUTERONOMY
10:17), God who created all things (GENESIS 1:1), and
God as judge (PSALM 50:6; 58:11). *Theos* is the New
Testament name of God and a common translation for
the Hebrew *Elohim*. The names *Yahweh* and *Adonai* mean
"lord." The name *Jehovah* is an artificial word created by
combining the vowels of *Adonai* with the consonants
YHWH. Christ is called God in the New Testament

(JOHN 1:1, 18, 20:28; 1 JOHN 5:20), and he's given the name that is above all names: "God exalted him to the highest place and gave him the name that is above every name, that at the name of Jesus every knee should bow, in heaven and on earth and under the earth, and every tongue confess that Jesus Christ is Lord" (PHILIPPIANS 2:6, 9–11). Christ also is called the Savior (1 TIMOTHY 1:1).

Finally, the Bible teaches that we worship one God in three persons: Father, Son, and Holy Spirit. The *Foundations* curriculum written by Tom Holladay and Kay Warren says the Bible teaches that God the Father, God the Son, and God the Holy Spirit are to be worshiped. The Father is God (JOHN 6:27; 1 PETER 1:2), the Son is God (JOHN 1:1, 18, 20:28; 1 JOHN 5:20; PHILIPPIANS 2:6, 9–11), and the Holy Spirit is God (ACTS 5:3–4). In the Trinity, God is one—not three gods, but one God (DEUTERONOMY 6:4). The three persons in the Trinity are distinct from one another— separate but one. Although it is a mystery we may not fully comprehend, it is a clear teaching of Scripture. Christians worship one God—the God of the Bible.

Keep writing, Lord.

Your story is beautiful.

LOGAN MUCHOW

Nº 2

WHAT IS THE HOLY SPIRIT'S ROLE
IN WORSHIP?

*M*any "worship services" are held, but worship doesn't always happen. One reason is that we sometimes fail to allow the Holy Spirit to fulfill his proper role in worship.

In honoring God the Father and lifting up Christ, we also must be careful to give proper place to the Holy Spirit.

God's Word says the Holy Spirit is "the Spirit of Jesus" (ACTS 16:7) and "the spirit of our God" (1 CORINTHIANS 6:11). He was involved in the creation of the world (GENESIS 1:2). He brought us the Bible (2 PETER 1:21). The Holy Spirit caused the Virgin Mary to conceive (LUKE 1:35). He guides us into truth (JOHN 16:13), convicts us of sin (JOHN 16:8), performs miracles (ACTS 8:39), and intercedes with God for us (ROMANS 8:26). He assures us that we belong to God as he "speaks to us deep in our hearts" (ROMANS 8:16 NLT).

The Holy Spirit is a living gift to all believers and is the divine source of spiritual power and ministry (JOHN 7:37–39;

It is the response of God's Spirit
in us to that Spirit in Him,
whereby we answer "Abba Father"
deep calling unto deep.

—PHILIP WENDELL CRANNELL

№ 3

HOW OLD DO YOU HAVE TO BE TO WORSHIP?

The Bible does not specify an age requirement to worship. In fact, the Scripture holds up children as examples of the kind of faith and humility necessary for authentic worship. God's Word teaches that little children sing praises to God, are model believers, and that God loves, protects, teaches, and calls them to serve like every other believer.

Jesus said, "Don't you know that the Scriptures say, 'Children and infants will sing praises'?" (MATTHEW 21:16 CEV). He was echoing an Old Testament passage that says God himself gives even the smallest child the ability to glorify him: "You have taught children and nursing infants to give you praise" (PSALM 8:2 NLT).

The faith of a child is precious to God and an example to the rest of us about genuine faith. Jesus said, "Let the little children come to me, and do not hinder them, for the kingdom of God belongs to such as these" (LUKE 18:16).

Youth is no barrier to serving God. Jeremiah was young when God called him into ministry: " 'Ah, Sovereign LORD,' I said. 'I do not know how to speak; I am only a child.' But the LORD said to me, 'Do not say, "I am only a child." You must go to everyone I send you to and say whatever I command you' " (JEREMIAH 1:6–7).

LET'S MAKE THREE OBSERVATIONS ABOUT CHILDREN AND WORSHIP.

First, children were present when Jesus spoke. For example, when the disciples asked who was the greatest in the kingdom of heaven, "he called a little child and had him stand among them" (MATTHEW 18:2). Not only were children present, they also were recognized as spiritual examples. Jesus continued, "I tell you the truth, unless you change and become like little children, you will never enter the kingdom of heaven" (MATTHEW 18:3). Childlike humility is absolutely essential to worship.

Further, the spiritual life of a child is a priority to Jesus. He said, "Whoever welcomes a little child like this in my name welcomes me" (MATTHEW 18:5). Welcoming children into worship is like welcoming the

Lord. Jesus also warns adults to be good witnesses to the children: "But if anyone causes one of these little ones who believe in me to sin, it would be better for him to have a large millstone hung around his neck and to be drowned in the depths of the sea" (MATTHEW 18:6). In the process, he presents children as being capable of believing in him.

Finally, the Bible documents children "walking in the truth" and serving in leadership. John wrote, "It has given me great joy to find some of your children walking in the truth, just as the Father commanded us" (2 JOHN 1:4). And we must mention that the Bible says, "The wolf will live with the lamb, the leopard will lie down with the goat, the calf and the lion and the yearling together; and a little child will lead them" (ISAIAH 11:6). Obviously, this Scripture prophesied specifically about the time of our Lord Jesus—a baby who changed the world!

HOW IMPORTANT IS WORSHIP TO CHILDREN?

A child's worship is significant and powerful. "Nursing infants gurgle choruses about you; toddlers shout the songs that drown out enemy talk, and silence atheist babble" (PSALM 8:2 MSG).

Congregations can help lay a solid foundation for the vitality of worship in the future by helping children worship from the earliest age. God uses the church to teach, encourage, and reinforce the practice of worship in our children. My church has been an invaluable help in raising my children to know and express their love to God.

THREE MORE OBSERVATIONS ABOUT CHILDREN AND WORSHIP:

First, Christ regarded children as exemplary worshipers: "At that time Jesus, full of joy through the Holy Spirit, said, I praise you, Father, Lord of heaven and earth, because you have hidden these things from the wise and learned, and revealed them to little children. Yes, Father, for this was your good pleasure" (LUKE 10:21). In fact, God teaches children to sing praises to Him: "Your name is the most wonderful name in all the earth! It brings you praise in heaven above. You have taught children and babies to sing praises to you" (PSALM 8:1–2 NCV).

Further, parents are responsible to teach and encourage their children to worship. The best worship class a parent can offer a child is a home with living examples of what it means to follow Christ. Children can sense authenticity and detect insincerity. Parents might have to make significant changes to align their lifestyles with what pleases God, but there is no other way to raise children before the Lord. It is much easier to live the truth than to attempt living a lie.

The Bible instructs parents: "Love the LORD your God with all your heart, soul, and strength. Memorize his laws and tell them to your children over and over again. Talk about them all the time, whether you're at home or walking along the road or going to bed at night, or getting up in the morning. Write down copies and tie them to your wrists and foreheads to help you obey them. Write these laws on the door frames of your homes and on your town gates" (DEUTERONOMY 6:5-9 CEV). Parents should do this naturally out of love for their children, but there also ought to be some measure of fear and obedience to God. Yes, fear! Consider Jesus' warning: "It would be better for him to be thrown into the sea with a millstone tied around his neck than for him to cause one of these little ones to sin" (LUKE 17:2).

Finally, like adults, children can worship through the way they live their lives. Choosing to build their lives on the foundation of God's principles is an act of worship. Children can worship by loving their parents, following the rules in class, sharing with their siblings, praying, giving, dancing, singing—and there are many more examples. In general, children can worship just by being themselves—full of life, energy, hope, tears, joy, love, trust, faith, questions, and even using their vivid, God–given imaginations.

CAN NONBELIEVERS WORSHIP?

Nonbelievers have a limited ability to worship. Because everyone is created by God to be a worshiper, everyone is able to worship something, but only Christians can truly worship God. "No one can say 'Jesus is Lord,' except by the Holy Spirit" (1 CORINTHIANS 12:3).

First, the Bible teaches that nonbelievers cannot worship God except in these two ways:

The instant of becoming a believer, when the nonbeliever listens to God and says "yes" to him (ACTS 28:28, 2 CORINTHIANS 5:17).

The instant when every knee bows to God at the Judgment (PHILIPPIANS 2:10).

Furthermore, everyone is born with a God–shaped hole in his or her heart. Nothing can satisfy the feeling of absolute emptiness, a hunger deep inside the heart, until the hole is filled with the Spirit of God. It is this

God–shaped hole that drives us to seek hi[m] [In other] words, God created each person from birt[h to be a] worshiper, and our souls will not rest unt[il we're] connected to God's Spirit. Like a computer searching for a secure WiFi connection, we are designed by God to keep searching until we find the connection to him, or until we're drained, like a battery, and shut down. People who do not worship God do worship something, but it is always something far less than the Master and Creator of the universe (2 CHRONICLES 7:22; DEUTERONOMY 11:16, 30:17; MATTHEW 6:24).

Finally, nonbelievers cannot truly worship during a church service; however, they can watch worship. My pastor, Rick Warren, often speaks of the evangelistic power of worship. He says:

Although unbelievers cannot truly worship, they can watch believers worship. They can observe the joy that we feel. They can see how we value God's Word and how we respond to it. They can hear how the Bible answers the problems and questions of life. They can notice how worship encourages, strengthens, and changes us. They can sense when God is supernaturally moving in a service, although they won't be able to explain it. When unbelievers watch genuine worship, it becomes a powerful witness.

The Bible teaches that as a nonbeliever observes genuine, authentic worship, God will speak to his or her heart. "But if some unbelieving outsiders walk in on a service where people are speaking out God's truth, the plain words will bring them up against the truth and probe their hearts. Before you know it, they're going to be on their faces before God, recognizing that God is among you" (1 CORINTHIANS 14:25 MSG).

DO WE REALLY WANT NONBELIEVERS TO ATTEND CHURCH?

This is an interesting question, and the answer depends on your view of the church. Consider this teaching from our doctrinal curriculum at Saddleback Church: "We are a part of his church and he involves us in building that church. But the moment it becomes ours rather than his, it's no longer a church."

First, the Bible teaches that the local church has very clear purposes. They are found in the Great Commandment (MATTHEW 22:37–40) and the Great Commission (MATTHEW 28:19–20):

1. Loving God with all your heart: Worship

2. Loving your neighbor as yourself: Ministry

3. Going and making disciples: Evangelism

4. Baptizing them into God's family: Fellowship

5. Teaching them to be "doers of the Word":
   Discipleship

Keeping these five purposes in mind, do you think God wants nonbelievers to attend your church?

Even though they can't engage in genuine, Spirit–led worship, they can watch your congregation worship; they can experience the love of your congregation; they can become disciples.

Furthermore, the Father loves nonbelievers and deeply desires to have a relationship with all of his children. "This is how much God loved the world: He gave his Son, his one and only Son. And this is why: so that no one need be destroyed; by believing in him, anyone can have a whole and lasting life. God didn't go to all the trouble of sending his Son merely to point an accusing finger, telling the world how bad it was. He came to help, to put the world right again" (JOHN 3:16–17 MSG). With God's great love in mind, do you think that God wants nonbelievers to attend church?

Finally, inviting nonbelievers to attend church is not about church growth or some trendy seeker movement; we are to invite nonbelievers to visit our churches because that's what God wants us to do. Being a "doer of the word" and not just a "hearer" (JAMES 1:22) includes obeying the Great Commandment and the Great

Commission. It's not enough to know these verses; they are a call to action from God, one that involves making choices: sacrifice over comfort, chaos over calm, service over "serve us," being available to do whatever it takes to serve God in our generation. As the saying goes, "Someone is waiting on the other side of your obedience." And through your obedience, Jesus will build the Church (MATTHEW 16:18).

A lukewarm heart cannot perform boiling hot worship, nor can a rebellious life revere God with any depth or sincerity.
–JUDSON CORNWALL

WHAT IS AN ACT OF WORSHIP?

*I*n *The Purpose Driven Life*, Rick Warren called surrender the heart of worship. "True worship—bringing God pleasure—happens when you give yourself completely to God," he said. I agree. Although actions can be a part of worship, it has much more to do with your perspective than what you are actually doing.

First, anything you do—that you've surrendered to his truth—can be an act of worship. That means anything from sharing your faith to playing with your children to enjoying your favorite movie can be an act of worship if you are living in total surrender to God.

Music can be an act of worship—but it doesn't have to be. When we roll into church on Sunday morning and sing a song just to check off another item on our to-do list, that's not worship. It's just singing. On the other hand, taking a nap—when we've surrendered control over all of the unmanageable events of life, when we've relaxed into the all-powerful hands of our Lord—can be a powerful statement of worship, particularly in a world that constantly relates busyness to value.

Further, obedience is an act of worship. One of the Hebrew words for "worship" is *abad*, which refers to working or serving as when a slave serves a master. Worship in scripture tied closely to that concept. To worship God is to do what he asks of us. Yet unlike slaves, we serve our Master out of gratitude and love.

Finally, surrender is an act of worship. It's worship when we surrender our own misguided ideas about our purpose and instead accept God's vision of what we were made for, including God's four other eternal purposes for our life: fellowship, spiritual maturity, ministry, and evangelism. Worship is the beginning, middle, and the culmination of the purpose–driven life. When we surrender our lives to the care of our spiritual family, the Church, when we make decisions that reveal how we are becoming more like Jesus, when we use our S.H.A.P.E.—Spiritual Gifts, Heart, Abilities, Personality, Experiences—to serve others, and when we tell others what God has done in our lives, we are worshiping.

Want to worship God? Live your life as God intended you to live it. Give up your plan and accept his. That means giving to God the ultimate act of worship— the surrender of your life to his purposes (ROMANS 12:1).

Worship is our response, both personal and corporate, to God for who He is and what He has done, expressed in and by the things we say and the way we live.

–LOUIE GIGLIO

WHEN SHOULD WE WORSHIP?

Christians should worship every day and should gather regularly for fellowship. Not just on Sundays. What if the week was ten days long? Would we worship every ten days? What if we missed a week? Then we would be worshiping every twenty days or so. That wouldn't make for a very close relationship with God.

We should worship whenever we are in God's presence. And when does that happen?

We live every moment of our lives in God's presence. Whether we are working or playing, eating or sleeping, minding our manners or misbehaving—God is right there. Paul told the debaters in Athens that in God "we live and move and have our being" (ACTS 17:28). The psalmist said there's nowhere we can go to get away from God—not into the darkness, not across the ocean, not even into the depths of hell (PSALM 139:7–12).

Hebrews 13:15 says, "Through Jesus, therefore, let us *continually* offer to God a sacrifice of praise—the fruit of lips that confess his name." If you think worship is something that happens only in a specific place at a definite time when you are doing a particular thing, then the idea of continually worshiping will strike you as strange. But if we should worship whenever we are in God's presence—and if we are always in God's presence—then we ought to worship *all the time.*

Brother Lawrence, who lived in a seventeenth–century Carmelite religious community, talked about "practicing the presence" of God. He realized that he was always in the Almighty's presence, whether he was kneeling at the altar or washing dishes. When it finally dawns on us that we are continually in God's presence—no matter where we are or what we are doing—our lives are completely transformed. Even the most mundane parts of our daily routines can become holy moments as we perform those chores "as unto the Lord."

Consider these three additional thoughts about when we should worship.

First, if worship is bringing pleasure to God, when wouldn't we want to worship? The Bible says, "I will praise the LORD at all times. His praise is always on my lips.

My whole being praises the LORD" (PSALM 34:1–2 NCV). It's not impossible, and you don't have to be a super spiritual person to worship continually. The fact is, we can bring glory to God regardless of what we are doing—as long as what we are doing honors him. God's Word says, "And we pray this in order that you may live a life worthy of the Lord and may please him in every way: bearing fruit in every good work, growing in the knowledge of God" (COLOSSIANS 1:10).

Further, does the Bible say which particular day we should go to church? The commandments God gave Moses instructed the people to observe a holy day on the seventh day of the week, resting from their labors as God himself did (EXODUS 20:8). The early Christians met together on "the first day of the week" because that was the day Christ rose from the dead. In addition, the risen Christ visited the disciples several times on the first day of the week (JOHN 20:1). Paul told the believers at Corinth that "on the first day of the week" they should set aside a sum of money in keeping with their income (1 CORINTHIANS 16:2). Although we know when early Christians *did* meet, the Bible doesn't mandate a specific day when we *must* meet. In fact, God's Word cautions us not to impose our beliefs about a worship day on those who have different convictions: "One man considers one day more sacred than another; another man considers every day alike. Each one should be fully convinced in his own mind" (ROMANS 14:5). The fact that we're meeting together is more important than which day we meet. Christians are to worship every day in everything and gather regularly with other believers (HEBREWS 10:25).

Finally, Jesus told the Samaritan woman at the well, "a time is coming, and it is already here! Even now the true worshipers are being led by the Spirit to worship the Father according to the truth. These are the ones the Father is seeking to worship him" (JOHN 4:23 CEV). That one verse answers four vital questions about worship: *Who?* The believer. *What?* The Father. *When?* The present. *Where?* In the spirit of each believer, where the Holy Spirit lives and leads.

When should you worship? *Now* is the time to worship!

Breathe a prayer of worship to God right now:

Father God, I am awed by the thought that you allow me to live in your presence. Jesus, I am grateful that you are in our midst when we gather in your name. Holy Spirit, I thank you that you are living in my heart. Lord, may I live each moment of my life in a manner that is worthy of you and always pleasing in your sight. Amen.

Nº 9

WHERE SHOULD WE WORSHIP?

We who believe are carefully joined together with Christ
as parts of a beautiful, constantly growing temple for God!
EPHESIANS 2:21 TLB

When we have an encounter with God, the place where we met him becomes very special to us. One such place for me is the sanctuary of our church building. Even if it is dark and empty, I sense God's presence. Memories of wonderful worship experiences flood my soul. But worship is more about relationship than about place.

A Samaritan woman talking with Jesus once raised the issue of where to worship: "Sir, I can see that you are a prophet. Our fathers worshiped on this mountain, but you Jews claim that the place where we must worship is in Jerusalem." Jesus replied, "Believe me, woman, a time is coming when you will worship the Father neither on this mountain nor in Jerusalem. . . . Yet a time is coming and has now come when the true worshipers will worship the Father in spirit and truth, for they are the kind of worshipers the Father seeks. God is spirit, and his worshipers must worship in spirit and in truth" (JOHN 4:19–21, 23–24).

First, notice that Jesus answered the "where" question by saying "in spirit and in truth." The believer's spirit is his essence, the very core of his being. The Great Commandment tells us to love the Lord with all our heart, soul, mind, and strength. Truth is the freedom we experience in genuine worship under a new covenant. We are not enslaved by a list of rules and regulations about worship. Instead, the Holy Spirit lives inside each believer, and we are able to worship wherever we are, outside a church building as well as in one. Worship is not limited to a place, because we live every moment in the presence of Holy God.

Further, believers need to worship with other believers. Hebrews 10:25 says, "Let us not give up meeting together, as some are in the habit of doing, but let us encourage one another, and all the more as you see the Day approaching." Romans 12:4–5 says, "Just as each of us has one body with many members, and these members do not all have the same function, so in Christ we who are many form one body, and each member belongs to all the others." We belong to each other! Church is a family, not a building. It is an organism, not an organization. Many churches around the world do not meet in buildings. Saddleback Church did not have its own building until it was ten years old and had five thousand attendees. The local church is Christ's precious bride: "Christ loved the church and gave his life for it" (Ephesians 5:25 cev). The important thing about worship is that we are complete when we are together—and Christ is pleased to be in our midst (Matthew 18:20).

Finally, every believer needs to commit to a local church body:

1. Where the teaching and preaching is scripturally accurate.

2. Where they can mature spiritually.

3. Where they can serve using their unique talents, spiritual gifts, experiences, passion, and personality.

4. Where there is a vision and a commitment to fulfilling the Great Commission and the Great Commandment.

5. Where the individual believer resonates with the leadership's philosophy of ministry.

6. Where God leads: "Trust in the LORD with all your heart; do not depend on your own understanding. Seek his will in all you do, and he will direct your paths" (PROVERBS 3:5–6 NLT).

Never rush into a decision about committing to a church, but don't wait too long either. There is no such thing as a perfect church, but every believer needs to belong to a congregation because the local church is God's family: "You are members of God's very own family, citizens of God's country, and you belong in God's household with every other Christian" (EPHESIANS 2:19 TLB).

WHY SHOULD WE WORSHIP?

"We love because God loved us first."
1 JOHN 4:19 CEV

*I*t may sound simple, but we worship God because we love God, and we love God because God first loved us.

We were made in the image of the perfect love between God the Father, Son, and Spirit (GENESIS 1:26), created to love and to be loved. God designed us to be at home in his perfect love, and it is God's love in us that compels us to love him and to love others: "Since God so loved us, we also ought to love one another" (1 JOHN 4:11).

Through Christ, God enters into a very personal union with each of us, not conceptually, not theoretically, not metaphorically . . . but ACTUALLY! He makes the first move to bridge the huge gap between the holy and the sinful, between his perfect love and our flawed love. Through Jesus, God established forever that genuine love is always personal—from a Person through a Person to a person.

Because the love of God is intimate and personal, the love flowing from you back to him—your worship of him—should be equally intimate and personal.

God's love doesn't stop at diagnosing our problems or judging our faults (PSALM 103:10); rather he moves to address the needs of our broken lives. Through worship, God brings fullness where there once was emptiness (COLOSSIANS 2:9–10); he brings life where there once was death (EPHESIANS 2:1, 5); he brings reconciliation where there once was separation (ROMANS 5:10–11).

To truly and deeply believe that God is perfectly loving us is the truth that sets us free from self–consciousness and self–absorption (ROMANS 12:2). As we embrace this love from God, we are drawn to worship him in a real and authentic way, the way we would be drawn to those we love the most.

The more we are conscious of God's love for us, the less self–conscious we become. Love begins to set the course of our lives, and worship becomes a natural outpouring of our transformed hearts.

When you recognize God's awesomeness,

it will evoke a certain response from you because

you see something and Someone

who is different and higher than you are.

To worship is to act as an inferior

before a superior.

−JOSEPH L. GARLINGTON

HOW CAN WE KNOW WHAT GOD IS REALLY LIKE?

The nature of God is one of history's most profound questions. In every age, in every corner of the world, men and women have wondered how to comprehend the mind of their Creator. Before we, as believers, can answer that age–old question, we must acknowledge an important truth: On our own we can know nothing about God; it's God who first reveals himself to us. We live in two different realms. God is so far above us in intellect and reason that we cannot even comprehend him unless he first explains himself to us (JOHN 1:18). Even if we were perfect creatures, the mind of God would be unreadable to us, but we are not perfect. Not only do our inferior minds keep us from knowing God, but our inferior hearts do as well. Our perception of the divine order has been forever dulled by sin and the power of the Evil One (2 CORINTHIANS 4:4).

Sometimes we get the idea that we can find out more about God through a discovery process in much the same way that scientists study the natural universe. But we can't. An ant could diligently study humans, but the insect would still be clueless when it comes to understanding who that person is.

The good news is that God didn't want to leave us like that. Because of his love for us, God chose to tell us more about himself; he chose to take the initiative in the relationship.

"For since the creation of the world God's invisible qualities—
his eternal power and divine nature—
have been clearly seen, being understood from what
has been made, so that men are without excuse."
ROMANS 1:20

First, we can look around and get a picture of God through nature and our experiences. We can see God's might by looking at the vastness of the sky and pondering the beauty of the seas. Still, what we know about God through creation is limited. While nature tells us something about God, it's vague without proper interpretation. It's like if someone tried to speak to you in a language you hadn't studied since high school. You may be able to understand a few words per sentence, but you couldn't understand enough to comprehend all that was meant to be communicated. We can know more about God through reflecting on our own experiences than from observing nature. For example, we know of God's trustworthiness and faithfulness because of how he has dealt with us when we needed his help.

Further, to communicate with us even more clearly, God gave us his Word. Speaking audibly to some people and through his Spirit to others, God gave human authors his infallible Word through the books of the Bible. The Bible gives us much of what we know about God. Because scripture often interprets itself, it gives us a much clearer picture of who God is. Therefore we know God by what he says in his Word. We know that God is consistent, changeless, because Psalm 33:11 says, "The plans of the LORD stand firm forever, the purposes of his heart through all generations."

We can trust that promise because we accept that God has chosen to reveal himself through scripture.

Finally, by far the clearest way God has revealed himself to man is through Jesus. God came to Earth to show us who he is. John tells us, "No one has seen God at any time; the only begotten God who is in the bosom of the Father, [Jesus] has explained Him" (JOHN 1:18 NASB). Paul tells us that he was the "image of the invisible God" (COLOSSIANS 1:15 NASB). Want to know who God is? Want to know his character and personality? Get to know Jesus. Study how he dealt with the people, issues, and cultures of his day. That's who God is today.

Still, we must recognize that we will not know the personhood and character of God perfectly this side of heaven. Limited by human nature—even with the aid of creation, our life experiences, scripture, and Jesus— there is an enormous amount about God and how he works in the world that we cannot know on this side of eternity. But, Paul tells us, one day we will know these answers, and we will know him perfectly.

"For now we see in a mirror dimly,
but then face to face; now I know in part,
but then I will know fully just as
I also have been fully known."

1 CORINTHIANS 13:12 NASB

HOW DO CHRISTIANS WORSHIP GOD?

*E*veryone worships something. We are born worshipers. God created us to worship.

Not everyone worships God, however. We can choose to worship people, things, power, pleasure, wealth, or anything else. But insight on worship can be gained even from that kind of worship.

Just for fun, consider people who worship sports. "Fans" (short for "fanatics") are known for their great passion for their team, an athlete, or even the city the team represents. Fans invest significant amounts of time and money to express their worship. They attend games to experience the thrill of victory and the agony of defeat. They shout praise: "Way to go!" or "We're number one!" They study the rules of the game, talk about the sport with anyone who will listen, learn statistics, teach the game to their children, wear the team colors, know players' names and numbers, and show loyalty against opponents. Fans love sports. Their intense devotion becomes worship.

God worship is very different from sports worship. God does not exist to entertain us or to serve us. He is holy. Our lives are in his hands—both now and in eternity. When God says he loves us he really means it. He gave up everything to prove it. God is not playing a game.

How can we worship God? Ephesians 5:10 tells us, "Figure out what will please Christ, and then do it" (MSG).

First, make God the primary focus of your daily life. The gateway to worship is making God most important in our lives. Jesus said, "Your heart will always be where your treasure is" (MATTHEW 6:21 CEV). When God is first, you will be eager to worship. "My heart tells me to pray. I am eager to see your face" (PSALM 27:8 CEV). Your most genuine worship will reflect the uniqueness of your life. God takes pleasure in you being who he created you to be. The Bible says, "So here's what I want you to do, God helping you: Take your everyday, ordinary life—your sleeping, eating, going-to-work, and walking-around life—and place it before God as an offering. . . . Don't become so well-adjusted to your culture that you fit into it without even thinking. Instead, fix your attention on God" (ROMANS 12:1–2 MSG). If you put on an act to fit in with other worshipers, you've stopped worshiping.

Further, Christian worship includes activity as much as it does attitude. Physical acts of worship—kneeling, singing, dancing, lifting hands, playing music, silence, giving—symbolize who owns your heart, who captivates your mind, who holds your soul, and who benefits from your strength. And the activity is not just what you do in church. In *The Purpose Driven Life*, Rick Warren says, "Every human activity, except sin, can be done for God's pleasure." Worship reaches out to take in every aspect of your daily life—not just attending church and praising God but also studying the Word, explaining the faith to others, dressing in a way that speaks well of God, showing loyalty, living a lifestyle of integrity, and helping people in need. These activities are outward expressions of deep inward realities. Accompanied by faith and obedience to God's Word, they are transformed from mere acts to authentic expressions of love, gratitude, and incredible joy over belonging to a great God and being a part of God's family!

Finally, worship begins in humility before God. Acknowledging our own unworthiness goes hand in hand with recognizing that he alone is worthy. Confession and repentance remove barriers to worship. The Bible says, "If I had not confessed the sin in my heart, my Lord would not have listened" (PSALM 66:18 NLT). "Come near to God, and he will come near to you. Clean up your lives, you sinners. . . . Be humble in the Lord's presence, and he will honor you" (JAMES 4:8, 10 CEV). Does sin in our lives really matter to God? Yes! Sin on the heart is like plaque on your teeth. It dims the worship experience and poses a serious long–term health problem. Before worshiping, ask God to search your heart and test your thoughts to see if there is any sin in your life (PSALM 139:23). When he reveals something, quickly agree with God that his way is better than your way and turn to walk with him.

my LiFe & will WORSHIP YoU

Lord, You've searched me

And You know me

You know when I sit and when I rise

You know my thoughts from far away

There's nothing hidden from Your eyes

Before I was born You saw me

Your love wrote the pages of my destiny

In every thing I do

I can worship You

I was created to

These hands that You have made

Are instruments of praise

My life will worship You.

—RICK MUCHOW

HOW CAN WE ENGAGE
ALL FIVE SENSES IN WORSHIP?

Our senses complement each other and help us interpret difficult concepts that lead us to a greater understanding of God. Have you ever noticed how things often taste like they smell, or look like they sound, or feel like they look? In nature God engages all five of our senses. And everyday places like restaurants, theme parks, shopping malls, and rock concerts come alive to us through our senses. Senses even affect learning styles. Some people are more visual, for example, while others learn best from hands–on experience.

God speaks to all five senses in worship. Music is an obvious way to worship by using our sense of hearing, and here's how we can engage our senses of sight, taste, touch, and smell.

SIGHT

Sight is powerful. Imagine the first time you saw your favorite painting or a depiction of Jesus on the cross.

Think of all the ways light affects our lives.
The Bible says Christians are to let our light shine
before the people of the world so that they may see
our good deeds and praise the Father in heaven
(MATTHEW 5:16). Obviously we use sight in worship,
such as when we read the Bible, but we also can engage
our sense of sight more intentionally. The expression
on a speaker or singer's face affects our worship.
Likewise, pictures and video images can present profound
truths in a memorable way. Photos of my children
impact me every time I look at them. They evoke
wonderful emotions and memories. Think of how
pictures used in worship can inspire believers to greater
levels of commitment and trigger truths they hold deep
in our hearts.

TASTE

Is it possible to use our sense of taste in worship?
Yes! Every one of our senses has a direct connection to the
brain. We taste the wine and wafer as we remember our
Lord during communion. And taste helps us understand
spiritual concepts. Psalm 34:8 says, "Taste and see that

the Lord is good." Obviously it doesn't mean that we physically taste the Lord, but we hunger for that which tastes good. And we hunger for the Lord. Food that tastes good gets our attention, and God is food for our souls. He says, "I am the bread of life. He who comes to me will never go hungry, and he who believes in me will never be thirsty" (John 6:35).

Touch

Like taste, touch is engaged metaphorically in worship. When we feel "touched" by the Lord we are having a spiritual experience, not a physical one. God also uses our physical bodies to touch a world with physical needs. Hugs represent love, brotherhood, and friendship. Touch is a very real expression of love and is an extension of the heart. Touch connects one soul to another. The laying on of hands for healing, anointing, commissioning, and showing compassion is an outward expression of a deep spiritual connection. Another way that God uses touch in worship is through music. It's the touch of a skillful musician that brings life to the instrument and excellence to the music, creating something beautiful that resonates with those who hear it. We are God's instruments. The touch of God's hand on our life is like that of the Master Musician, "because he himself gives all men life and breath and everything else" (ACTS 17:25).

SMELL

Smell indicates a sense of presence. When people smell something, they don't have to see it to know that it's really there. Many churches use candles to remind worshipers that they worship a God who is Spirit and cannot be seen but is with us. Smell can indicate the quality of something. When something smells good—like food, a pillow, a puppy, the air we breathe—it is perceived as clean, healthy, good, and desirable. The Bible says, "Our lives are a fragrance presented by Christ to God. But this fragrance is perceived differently by those being saved and by those perishing" (2 CORINTHIANS 2:15 NLT). Other verses describe the aroma of unacceptable worship. Nobody, including God, enjoys a bad smell.

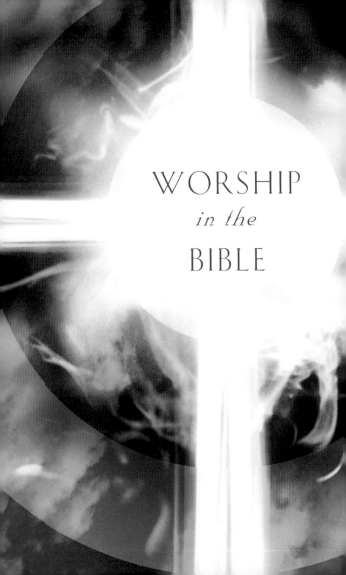

WORSHIP
in the
BIBLE

The Bible is a reflection of the mind of God, and in his Word he teaches us about himself and the best ways we can worship him. This section digs deeper into the meanings and methods of worship.

"Worship and serve [God] with your whole heart
and with a willing mind. For the LORD sees every heart
and understands and knows every plan and thought.
If you seek him, you will find him.
But if you forsake him, he will reject you forever."

1 CHRONICLES 28:9 NLT

WHAT DOES THE WORD 'WORSHIP' MEAN?

I was surprised to learn that the word "worship" is used only 108 times in the King James Version of the Bible and 158 times in the New International Version.

In English, "worship" means to greatly love, admire, or respect somebody or something and to show it by engaging in acts of prayer and devotion. Worship is the way people show their devotion to God—or to something they have put in God's place.

The Bible, however, was originally written in Hebrew (Old Testament) and Greek (New Testament), languages that can be much richer in texture than English. English translations of the Bible use a single word, "worship," to communicate the meanings of four different Hebrew words and six different Greek words, but each of those Hebrew and Greek words carries a specific meaning that offers greater insight into the meaning of worship.

The Old Testament uses four words that are translated "worship" in English:

Shachah (shaw–khaw) means "to bow down." Strong's Greek and Hebrew Dictionary says it means "to depress, i.e., prostrate (especially reflexive in homage to royalty or God)—bow (self) down, crouch, fall down (flat), humbly beseech, do (make) obeisance, do reverence, make to stoop, worship." *Shachah* is translated "worship" forty–seven times in the Bible. "We will worship" (GENESIS 22:5).

Abad (aw–bahd) means "to work or serve." Strong's defines it as "to work (in any sense); by implication to serve, (causative) enslave, etc. (cause to, make to) serve (–ing, self), (be, become) servant (–s), do (use) service, (set a) work, worshiper." *Abad* is used in Deuteronomy 6:13: "You shall fear only the LORD your God; and you shall worship Him and swear by His name" (NASB). Of the 290 times *abad* is used in the Bible, it is translated "serve" 227 times.

Paneh (paw–neem) is a root word used 2,109 times in the Bible. It means "face" 390 times and "before" 1,137 times. *Panim* can be a substitute for the self or the feelings of the self. In I Kings 12:30 it is used regarding "facing" (worshiping) false gods. *Paneh* is most frequently used as a preposition: "in the presence of," "before." *Paneh* is an invitation to worship God.

Segid (sih–geed) means "to show reverence and respect to somebody." One of the twelve times this word is used is in Daniel 3:5: "that at the moment you hear the sound of the horn, flute, lyre, trigon, psaltery, bagpipe and all kinds of music, you are to fall down and worship the golden image" (NASB). This word is used for worship of God, idols, and men.

Six words in the New Testament are translated into English as "worship:"

Proskuneo (prah–skoo–neh–oh) is the word used in the wise men's declaration in Matthew 2:2: "Where is the one who has been born king of the Jews? We saw his star in the east and have come to worship him." Also translated "bow down," it means "to show reverence, to adore." This word appears in John 4:24: "God is spirit, and his worshipers must worship in spirit and in truth."

Sebomai (seh–bohm–ahee) means "to revere, adore—devout, religious worship," according to Strong's Greek and Hebrew Dictionary. One of its ten uses is in Matthew 15:9: "They worship me in vain."

Doxa (doh–ksah) gave us our word "doxology." Used 168 times, *doxa* means "dignity, glory (–ious), honor, praise, and worship." The only time it is translated "worship" is in the Gospel of Luke: "But when thou art bidden, go and sit down in the lowest room; that when he that bade thee cometh, he may say unto thee, Friend, go up higher: then shalt thou have worship in the presence of them that sit at meat with thee" (LUKE 14:10 KJV). A well–known *doxa* verse is Philippians 2:11—"And that every tongue should confess that Jesus Christ is Lord, to the glory of God the Father."

Latreuo (lah–tree–oo–oh) is another very important word. It means "to serve, to minister." This word is used twenty–one times, including in Philippians 3:3: "For we are the circumcision, which worship God in the spirit, and rejoice in Christ Jesus, and have no confidence in the flesh" (KJV).

Eusebeo (you–seh–beh–oh) means "to reverence or show piety to those whom it is due." The word appears in Paul's sermon in Athens: "You worship this God, but you don't really know him. So I want to tell you about him" (ACTS 17:23 CEV). In I Timothy 5:4, *eusebeo* is used to express the responsibility of service that children and grandchildren have toward their families.

Ethelothreskia (eth–el–oh–thray–skay–ah) means "self–willed (arbitrary and unwarranted) piety . . . self–made religion," according to the NASB dictionary. Colossians 2:23 uses the word like this: "Which things have indeed a show of wisdom in will–worship and humility, and neglecting of the body, not in any honor to the satisfying of the flesh" (KJV). The New Century Version says it this way: "These rules seem to be wise, but they are only part of a man–made religion *(Ethelothreskia)*."

You can enrich your understanding of Scripture by studying the meanings of Hebrew and Greek words. Resources include sites like speedbibledictionary.com, books like *Strong's Hebrew and Greek Dictionary*, and computer programs like WordSearch Bible software.

THE WORSHIP SONG

Hallelujah, praise the Lord
Maranatha, come quickly, Lord
Hosanna, save us now
Abba, Father
Amen, let it be so

We worship you
We worship you
We worship you
By grace, through faith

Let the Amen
Sound from his people again
Let it be so!

—Rick Muchow

This song was inspired by the five universal words of worship. When a friend first explained these words to me, I was surprised that I knew so little about worship. Now, as a commitment to further study and a constant reminder to live a life of worship, I wear a ring with all five of these amazing words engraved on it.

WHAT DO OTHER BIBLICAL TERMS
RELATED TO WORSHIP MEAN?

Abba—Aramaic word meaning "Father." This name implies childlike trust (MARK 14:36).

Adonai—Hebrew word meaning "lord, master, and owner." Conveys the idea of absolute authority (JOSHUA 5:14). Combined with the consonants of YHWH produces the word "Jehovah."

Alleluia—Greek word meaning "Praise the Lord!" *Halal* means to boast, *Jah* (YAH) is the sacred name for the Lord (REVELATION 19:1). Same meaning as the Hebrew word *hallelujah*.

Amen—Hebrew word meaning "so be it" or "let it be so" (NUMBERS 5:22). It pronounces that what was said, or what's about to be said, is dependable, faithful, and certain. It is related to a Hebrew word meaning "believe" and is an expression of absolute trust and confidence.

Barak—Hebrew word meaning "to bow or kneel in reverence to God" (PSALM 72:15).

El Elyon—Hebrew word meaning "the most high God" (strength, sovereignty, and supremacy) (GENESIS 14:9).

Elohim—Hebrew name of God meaning "the strong one, the mighty leader, the supreme deity" (GENESIS 1:1).

El Olam—Hebrew word meaning "the Everlasting God," God is unchanging (PSALM 100:5).

El Roi—Hebrew word meaning "the God who sees" (knows the future) (GENESIS 16:13).

El Shaddai—Hebrew word that pictures God as the Almighty One standing on a mountain: "Comforter and Judge" (PSALM 91:1–2).

Hallelujah—Hebrew word that means "Praise the Lord"; *Halal* means "to boast," *Jah* (YAH) is the sacred name for the Lord (REVELATION 19:1). Same meaning as the Greek word *alleluia*.

Hosanna—This is a Greek transliteration of a Hebrew word. It means "save us" or "save now." It was customarily used at the Feast of Tabernacles and is a shout of welcome and adoration (MATTHEW 21:9).

Immutability—Word that means God will never change or be changed (MALACHI 3:6).

Kana (kaw–NAH)—Hebrew word meaning "to be humble" or "to subdue." Often used to describe "subduing" an enemy, it is also used "to humble oneself" before God (2 CHRONICLES 7:14).

Maranatha—Aramaic or Syrica word meaning "our Lord comes" or "our Lord is coming" (1 CORINTHIANS 16:22). It is used to add solemn emphasis to a previous statement.

Master (Despotes)—Greek word offering the idea of ownership (LUKE 2:29; 2 PETER 2:1).

Omnipotence—Word that means God is all–powerful and able to do anything he chooses (EXODUS 6:3).

Omnipresence—Word that means God is everywhere at the same time (PSALM 139:7–11).

Omniscience—Word that means God knows everything (PSALM 139:16).

Selah—Hebrew musical term most likely meaning "pause"; it appears seventy–one times in Psalms (PSALM 3:2).

Shabah—Word meaning "praise" or "glorify" (PSALM 63:3) using a loud voice.

Tehillah—Hebrew word meaning glory; praise; a song of praise or hymn (PSALM 100).

Todah—Hebrew word for "praise"; same as *yadah* but done with a congregation or choir of worshipers (PSALM 42:4).

Yadah—Hebrew word for "praise" or "thanks"; "to hold out the hands" and "to confess, praise, and give thanks" (PSALM 9, 105:1).

YHWH—Hebrew word for the personal name of God, pronounced *yah-way* or *Juh-hove-ah*; (Genesis 2:4); "Jehovah" is an artificial word produced by combining the vowels of *Adonai* with the consonants of *YHWH* (PSALM 83:18).

Zamar—Hebrew word for musical praise, either instrumental or singing (PSALM 104:33).

IS THERE A BIBLICAL MUSICAL STYLE?

*T*he Bible does not have an official soundtrack. Many different musical styles were expressed over the millennia during which the Bible's books were written. Sacred song lyrics are recorded throughout the Bible, and several instruments are mentioned. We have a few clues about tempo, volume, and the purpose of the music, but there is little evidence as to the specific musical style in which those lyrics were performed—nor does it seem important.

No single music style is more biblical than another. In fact, many of the musical styles that have been popular in churches during the past two hundred years probably bear little resemblance to the styles that prevailed in biblical times. Musical styles reflect the cultures in which they arise—and modern cultures are dramatically different from the cultures of Abraham, Moses, David, and Jesus!

Some insight into the music of Bible times can be gained from archaeomusicology, also known as music archaeology, which is a discipline that specifically explores past music cultures through archaeological artifacts and historic texts. Scripture itself is an important example of such texts.

So what do we know about music in Bible times?

First, we can learn about the music of the Bible by looking at the instruments that were played. They include the human voice, horn, shofar (a ram's horn), trumpet, flute, lyre (plucked string instrument, U-shaped, several different string configurations), lute (like a guitar with a pear-shaped body and a flat front), trigon (three-sided harp or lyre), psaltery (stringed instrument that can be plucked or bowed), bagpipe, timbrel (tambourine), loud-sounding cymbals, castanets, and instruments made of fir wood (2 SAMUEL 6:5; JOB 21:12; PSALM 150:4; DANIEL 3:15).

We also know that Hebrew music was rendered in unison (2 CHRONICLES 5:13). There was no harmony; everyone played the same notes. This feature alone gives us an idea of what the music could have sounded like. Unison is not necessarily easier to play. It is actually more difficult to be in tune when playing in unison, but when a band plays this way, the music carries better outside. From a symbolic view, unison is a musical device that represents spiritual unity and oneness.

Finally, we learn about the music of that era from the setting described in Scripture. "Four thousand were praising the Lord with the instruments which David made for giving praise" (1 CHRONICLES 23:5 NASB). Obviously, they had some large gatherings—if four thousand people were in the band! Second Chronicles 5:13 tells about cymbals, harps, lyres, and 120 priests blowing trumpets in unison. The music must have been very loud. The singers were "clothed in fine linen"— obviously they had a dress code. I love involving all the talent in worship! On the other hand, a much more intimate sound is implied by the performance instructions that precede some of the Psalms: "For the choir director, with stringed instruments upon an eight–stringed lyre" (PSALM 6 NASB). The words of the psalm are intimate and most likely were accompanied by an appropriately sensitive style of music from the lyre.

Likewise, Isaiah 38:20 says, "We will play my songs on stringed instruments all the days of our life at the house of the LORD" (NASB). Playing with skill and joy is a consistent instruction (1 SAMUEL 16:16, 18:6).

While each of us may prefer one musical style over another, there is no such thing as one biblical musical style. I suspect that when God listens to our music, he is most concerned about what is in our hearts. Although God loves music, he loves us more!

In the same way, our love for a certain type of music should pale in comparison to our love for God. Romans 12:2 reminds us to not become so adjusted to human culture that we allow it to dictate how we serve God. Instead, we are told to fix our attention on God.

It's a fact that God loves us more than he loves our music, and we are to love others in the same way. Our musical style is never as important to God as the key we play it in—and love is the key.

I have no objection to instruments

of music in our chapels

provided they are neither heard nor seen.

–JOHN WESLEY

HOW WAS GOD WORSHIPED
IN THE OLD TESTAMENT?

God never changes, and neither does the heart of worship. The external forms of worship may have varied from the Old Testament to the New Testament, but glorifying God has always been the same.

A look at the Scripture shows us that worship in the Old Testament, like today, was done in public settings (1 CHRONICLES 29:20, PSALM 42:4), individually (GENESIS 24:26, EXODUS 34:8), and as families (GENESIS 8:20, GENESIS 22:5). Public worship in the temple involved sacrifices (2 CHRONICLES 7:5), ceremonial acts and a posture of reverence (2 CHRONICLES 7:6), instrumental or vocal praise (2 CHRONICLES 5:13), spoken praise (1 CHRONICLES 16:36), public prayer (DEUTERONOMY 26), and annual feasts (PSALM 42:4).

But authentic worship has never been a matter of mere outward expressions. Acceptable worship in the Old Testament required repentance of sin, humility, sincere faith in God alone, and hope in his Messiah.

Worship to impress others or for any selfish reason was as unacceptable then as it is now.

Psalm 96 gives us a good feel for the heart of Old Testament worship:

> "Sing GOD a brand–new song! Earth and
> everyone in it, sing! Sing to GOD—worship
> GOD! Shout the news of his victory from sea
> to sea, take the news of his glory to the lost,
> news of his wonders to one and all! For GOD
> is great, and worth a thousand Hallelujahs.
> His terrible beauty makes the gods look cheap;
> pagan gods are mere tatters and rags. GOD
> made the heavens—royal splendor radiates
> from him, a powerful beauty sets him apart.
> Bravo, GOD, Bravo! Everyone join in the great
> shout: Encore! In awe before the beauty, in awe
> before the might. Bring gifts and celebrate,
> bow before the beauty of GOD, Then to your
> knees—everyone worship! Get out the
> message—GOD Rules! He put the world on a
> firm foundation. He treats everyone fair and

square. Let's hear it from Sky, with Earth
joining in, and a huge round of applause from
Sea. Let Wilderness turn cartwheels, Animals,
come dance, put every tree of the forest in the
choir—an extravaganza before GOD as he comes,
as he comes to set everything right on earth,
set everything right, treat everyone fair" (MSG).

When I study the Old Testament, I notice three
vibrant characteristics of worship.

First, worship is consistently tied to *joy*. The Psalms
clearly reflect joyous worship: "I will give thanks to the
LORD with all my heart; I will tell of all your wonders.
I will be glad and exult in you" (PSALM 9:1–2 NASB).
God's love of joyful celebration is evident in the fact
that there are more than ninety feast days on the Jewish
religious calendar.

Further, Old Testament worship involved *response*—
the soul fulfilling its God–given purpose! Deeds and
posture were as much a part of worship as words
and dedication. Psalm 96 urges worshipers to tell, give
glory, tremble, and bring, as well as to sing, rejoice,

and shout. Did you notice the evangelistic emphasis? Old Testament worship was a telling faith!

Finally, Old Testament worship included *remembrance*. Praising the Lord is often connected to the reasons for that praise. Psalm 96 tells of believers celebrating what God had done for them in the past. God's people then and now praise him for the ways he has changed their lives and saved them from destruction.

> *The humblest and most unseen activity in the world can be the true worship of God.*
> —WILLIAM BARCLAY

HOW DID JESUS WORSHIP?

Does the idea of Jesus worshiping seem odd to you? After all, he was God himself (Philippians 2:6–7). He was one with the Father (John 10:30). Why did Jesus need to worship?

Well, the fact is, he did worship the Father. Speaking to the Samaritan woman, he said, "You Samaritans worship what you do not know; we worship what we do know" (John 4:22).

"We worship"—coming from Jesus—is an amazing statement to me. He knows he is God, that he and the Father are one, but he worships with his friends and doesn't use his identity to exalt himself. If anyone ever had a reason to be all about himself, it was Jesus, but instead he was totally about doing the will of his Father. His submission to the Father knew no limit: "Who (Christ), being in very nature God, did not consider equality with God something to be grasped, but made himself nothing, taking the very nature of a servant, being made in human likeness. And being

found in appearance as a man, he humbled himself and
became obedient to death—even death on a cross!"
(Philippians 2:6–7).

You can learn everything there is to know about
worship from studying the life of Christ. Here are some
examples of Jesus' worship life to begin your discovery.

- He prayed—Mark 1:35
- He taught—Mark 1:39, Luke 21:57
- He preached—Mark 1:38
- He was baptized—Mark 1:9
- He gave—Mark 12:17
- He resisted temptation—Luke 4:8
- He fasted—Matthew 4:2
- He obeyed the Father—Hebrews 12:2
- He read the Scripture—Matthew 21:42
- He quoted Scripture—Matthew 22:37
- He sang—Matthew 26:30
- He praised the Father—Matthew 11:25; John 12:28
- He worshiped daily—Mark 14:49
- His life was worship—Matthew 26:39

Continue your study of Jesus' worship life by trying these three things:

1. Read through the Gospels (Matthew, Mark, Luke, and John) and look for examples of how Jesus worshiped. Then challenge yourself to try to worship like he did.

2. Read through the entire New Testament looking for other references to the worship practices of Christ.

3. Make it a priority to practice humility and obedience—the essential character qualities of the worshiper.

The best worshipers are those who pattern their lives around Jesus' character qualities. We can best bring pleasure to God by becoming more like his Son, Jesus Christ. "I have set you an example that you should do as I have done for you" (JOHN 13:15).

WHAT DID JESUS TEACH
ABOUT WORSHIP?

Jesus' life is the supreme example of worship. He *is* the lesson. Everything Jesus did and said was a demonstration of true worship.

Jesus understood that because worship includes living a life that honors God, the way you respond to temptation has a profound impact on your worship. When the devil confronted him in the wilderness, Jesus responded by talking about worship: "You must worship the Lord your God; serve only him" (LUKE 4:8, NLT).

Jesus said the life of worship is a focused life characterized by prayer. In the Garden of Gethsemane, he told Peter: "Keep alert and pray. Otherwise temptation will overpower you. For though the spirit is willing enough, the body is weak" (MARK 14:38, NLT).

Jesus also taught that authentic worship flows from a heart filled with love for God. Quoting the prophet Isaiah, he said: "These people honor me with their lips, but their hearts are far away. Their worship is a farce, for they replace God's commands with their own man–made teachings" (MARK 7:7, NLT).

Consider these three additional thoughts about Jesus' teaching on worship.

First, the Sermon on the Mount (MATTHEW 5–7) is filled with lessons about worship. God blesses worshipers (5:3–12). Worshipers are salt and light to the world (5:13–16). Worshipers must obey God's commands (5:17–20). Anger impedes worship (5:21–26). Our thoughts matter (5:27–30). Worshipers keep their promises (5:33–37). Always love like your Father in heaven (5:43–48). Worship involves doing good deeds (6:1), giving (6:2), praying (6:9–13), forgiving (6:14), fasting (6:16–18), sticking to priorities (6:19–21), keeping money in perspective (6:24), living free from worry (6:25), not condemning others (7:1–5), asking God for good things (7:7–11), not seeking shortcuts to godliness (7:13–14), and watching out for false teachers (7:15–20). Worship is worthless without obedience (7:21–27).

Further, not only is prayer an act of worship, but the Lord's Prayer (MATTHEW 6:9–13) offers great insight into five themes of worship: "Our Father (*Abba*) which art in heaven, Hallowed (*Hallelujah*) be thy name. Thy kingdom come (*Maranatha*). Thy will be done in earth, as it is in heaven. Give us this day our daily bread. And forgive us our debts, as we forgive our debtors. And lead us not into temptation, but deliver us from evil (*Hosanna*): For thine is the kingdom, and the power, and the glory, forever. *Amen*" (KJV). There's a worship lesson in this prayer!

Finally, Jesus taught about worship by the way he lived his life. He completely fulfilled the will of the Father (JOHN 19:30). He faced all the same temptations we face, but he never sinned (1 PETER 2:22). He chose to worship God rather than giving into temptation (LUKE 4:8). He was baptized (LUKE 3:21-22). He was obedient to the Father by enduring the cross (HEBREWS 12:2). He observed the Sabbath and taught in the synagogue (MARK 6:2). Jesus meditated on Scripture (LUKE 2:46-47). He sang hymns (MATTHEW 26:30). Peter tells us: "This is the kind of life you've been invited into, the kind of life Christ lived. He suffered everything that came his way so you would know that it could be done, and also know how to do it, step by step" (1 PETER 2:21–22 MSG).

Additional teachings by Christ related to worship:

- Pray to God—Matthew 9:13, 9:38, 12:7, 14:23
- Welcome children—Matthew 19:13
- Love the Lord your God—Matthew 22:37
- Follow good teaching—Matthew 23:6
- Love the Lord your God—Mark 11:24, 12:30
- Watch out for false teachers—Mark 12:38
- Rebuke false holiness—Luke 11:42
- Jesus commands humility—Luke 11:43, 14:10
- No one can serve two masters—Luke 16:13
- Worship in spirit and truth—John 4:20–24
- Worshipers keep commandments—John 14:15
- Christ's presence is known by those who keep commandments—John 14:21
- Jesus warns of the consequences for worshiping God on this Earth—John 15:19
- Love is better than sacrifice—Mark 12:38

Nº 20

WHAT DID JESUS SAY ABOUT WORSHIP TO THE SEVEN CHURCHES MENTIONED IN REVELATION?

The Book of Revelation was written by John of Patmos, a pastor in the late first century and overseer of a string of churches whose preeminent focus was to be platforms of worship for early believers. Worship is an overarching topic of this book, which ranks as one of the most challenging parts of the Bible. It's jam-packed with allusion, metaphor, symbolism, and imagery, all depicting a dazzling picture of the epic culmination of events that occurs sometime in humanity's future. Yet Revelation's most important theme is unmistakably clear: worship, our response to God with all that we are, is central to human affairs both in the lives of individuals and to humanity at large.

First, Jesus' words to the seven churches in Revelation chapters 2 and 3 repeatedly pulse with a clear theme that people have to overcome the many malevolent forces at work in the world—including within the church and within ourselves—that come against worship. So much is at stake when it comes to humans and worship, and the Evil One and the forces seeking to undermine our world want worship to go awry. In its right state, worship is our response—individually and collectively—to a loving, living God who yearns to be close to us like a loving parent with a child. When worship is right, when the object of our worship is right and the motive for our worship is as it should be, then the order of the Creation is as it was intended to be. When that happens—and sometimes we do get glimpses of it—there is unspeakably beautiful fruit in our lives, in the lives of our churches, and even potentially in the world at large.

Further, when you list the things for which Jesus commends the seven churches and the issues for which he challenges them, you implicitly understand that the scope and dimension of worship is so much more than what happens in one hour on a Sunday morning. It has to do with every aspect of our lives—our relationships, our labor, our service, our deepest thoughts, our true intentions, all of it. The forces that come against worship include pride, idolatry, deception, fear, oppression, selfishness, hatred, exploitation, and self–indulgence. When those motivations reign in our lives, individually and/or corporately, our worship and our lives in general are profoundly and adversely affected. Conversely, Jesus commends the seven churches for virtues like faithfulness, meekness, service, courage, truth, persistence, authenticity, generosity, unity, and perseverance. When these attributes define who we are, both individually and corporately, then our worship and our lives will reap untold goodness.

Finally, just a few chapters later, the writer does his best to describe an unimaginably sacred and exquisite scene that will take place sometime in the future when people everywhere, "all nations and tribes, all races and languages" (REVELATION 7:9 MSG), finally understand who Jesus is and together worship him in a way that, given the state of our world and our troubled times, challenges our intellect and our collective hopes and aspirations and dreams. This unified worship is the dream God has for all people everywhere—a climactic scene of restoration and reconciliation between a loving Creator and his much-loved Creation. It is a fearless movement for an epic harmony we as believers are called to join. And it has everything to do with the heart of our worship—which has everything to do with how our very lives are shaped.

> *Serve and honor the LORD;*
> *be glad and tremble.*
> −PSALM 2:44

IS IT TRUE THAT ONE DAY EVERY PERSON WILL WORSHIP GOD?

Yes, the Bible tells us that one day every person, even those who have scorned him and rejected his gift of grace and salvation, will eventually fall to their knees before God.

Three passages in Scripture describe this:

Isaiah 45:23–25—"By myself I have sworn, my mouth has uttered in all integrity a word that will not be revoked: Before me every knee will bow; by me every tongue will swear. They will say of me, 'In the LORD alone are righteousness and strength.' All who have raged against him will come to him and be put to shame. But in the LORD all the descendants of Israel will be found righteous and will exult."

Romans 14:11—" 'As surely as I live,' says the Lord, 'every knee will bow before me; every tongue will confess to God.' " By quoting this passage from Isaiah, the Apostle Paul is reminding us that judging is God's job and not ours. "Who are you to judge someone else's servant?" (v. 4). "Why do you look down on your brother?" (v. 10). "Therefore let us stop passing judgment on one another" (v 13).

Philippians 2:10–11—Paul also writes that "at the name of Jesus everyone will bow down, those in heaven, on earth, and under the earth. And to the glory of God the Father everyone will openly agree, 'Jesus Christ is Lord' " (CEV). Throughout verses 1–18 of this chapter of Paul's letter, believers are reminded and encouraged to develop the attitude of Christ (humility), and to "work out your salvation with fear and trembling for it is God who works in you to will and to act according to his good purpose (judgment is coming) and to do everything without complaining."

I think the message of Isaiah 45:22–24 could be paraphrased like this: "I am God and there is no other. Turn to me while you are alive and be saved, or turn to me after you die and be put to shame. I am the only God and you will certainly worship me."

In one of the most famous passages in the entire Bible, God shows his compassion, asserts his sovereignty,

and warns of judgment for those who do not believe
before they die. God wants everyone to know him and
to be saved. "For this is how God loved the world: he
gave his only Son, so that everyone who believes in him
may not perish but may have eternal life" (JOHN 3:16 NJB).

These are among the passages that teach us not to
spend our time judging the spiritual condition of
others, but instead to look closely at our own spiritual
lives and to be "doers of the word," not hearers alone
(JAMES 1:22). Believers will be judged by God in the
same way that they judge others (MATTHEW 7:1–2).

At the Judgment, the Bible teaches that worshipers
will fall into one of three categories:

First, believers will worship and confess in the Lord
alone. Those who love God will bow in adoration and
worship, and God will judge their works. Jesus will say,
"My father has blessed you! Come and receive the
kingdom that was prepared for you before the world
was created" (MATTHEW 25:34 CEV).

Furthermore, people who refused to acknowledge
God and his Son, Jesus, will bow in submission and

fear at this final Judgment. "Those people will be punished forever" (MATTHEW 25:46 CEV). Much like a defeated army, nonbelievers will bow before the King of kings and confess that Jesus is Lord. They will do this not as grateful citizens but like a vanquished nation.

Finally, at this final Judgment the worshipers who are all talk and no action will be exposed as fraudulent, and for the first time they will truly worship God as they plead for their eternal lives. Jesus warned that not everyone who says, "Lord, Lord" will enter the kingdom of heaven, but only those who do the will of the "Father in heaven" (MATTHEW 7:21). "Many will say to me on that day, 'Lord, Lord, did we not prophesy in your name, and in your name drive out demons and perform many miracles?' Then I will tell them plainly, 'I never knew you. Away from me, you evildoers'" (MATTHEW 7:22–23).

These are sobering thoughts! The importance of worship takes on new gravity when considering how serious worship is to God and how eternity weighs in the balance. These scriptures show there is a difference between being a believer in God and simply believing that God exists. Satan believes that God exists, but he does not believe in—trust in—God (JAMES 2:19). May you allow God to examine your own heart as you grapple with the meaning of his love and grace, and may you trust in Jesus as your Lord and Savior if you have not done so already. My prayer is that you will become a "doer of God's Word" who is prepared for the final Judgment Day.

> *What you worship has a great influence*
> *on what you are. . . . You become*
> *like the god you worship.*
> –JACK HAYFORD

MORE THAN WORTHY

Lift up your voices
and let it be heard
The sound of the nations
in all of the earth
Alleluia, Alleluia

Lift up your hands
and raise to the King
Lift up your heart
as an offering sing
Alleluia, Alleluia

More than lovely
More than worthy
More than beautiful is the King
You're my Savior
You're my Friend
You're my wonderful and mighty God

And so we have risen to fall on our knees
To worship the Lamb whose death brought us peace
Alleluia, Alleluia

We lift up our hands and raise to the King
We lift up our hearts as an offering sing
Alleluia, Allelluia

© Brandon Muchow

PERSONAL
WORSHIP

The Bible is clear that everything we do, even the most ordinary acts of our lives, can become acts of worship when done in a spirit of service and humility. This section shows how to worship God continually throughout the day.

The LORD is my shepherd;
I have everything I need.
He lets me rest in green meadows;
he leads me beside peaceful streams.
He renews my strength.
He guides me along right paths,
bringing honor to his name.
Even when I walk
through the dark valley of death,
I will not be afraid,
for you are close beside me.
Your rod and your staff
protect and comfort me.
You prepare a feast for me
in the presence of my enemies.
You welcome me as a guest,
anointing my head with oil.
My cup overflows with blessings.
Surely your goodness and unfailing
love will pursue me
all the days of my life,
and I will live in the house of the
LORD forever.

PSALM 23 NLT

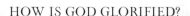

HOW IS GOD GLORIFIED?

All personal worship starts with remembering what worship is about—glorifying God.

God is glorified in much the same way as a bride is honored at her wedding.

The word "glorify" is derived from a Greek word, *doxazo*, which means "to render glorious." To glorify means to praise or magnify.

In a wedding, the bride is the focus of everyone's attention. The guests stand as she enters the room. She walks down the center aisle as the grand finale of the wedding party's processional. Her dress is by far the most expensive and elaborate. The women who accompany her are the "bridesmaids;" the man getting married is the "bridegroom." "Bridal party," "bridal march," "bridal shower." The bride is the most beautiful, most important, and most honored person of the day. Many gifts are given, but the real gift brought to the wedding is love.

When people are glorified—brides, rock stars, athletes, celebrities, politicians—they are made to look larger than they are. God, however, doesn't need to be larger. In fact, he can't be made larger than he already is—he's omnipotent, everywhere!—but he can be made larger in our lives. That is how God is glorified.

First, God is glorified by believers who show up. Wedding guests glorify the bride by attending the ceremony. Even if attending involves a significant personal cost, the guests have made the wedding a priority. The cost pales in significance to the great joy the wedding brings. The love outweighs the sacrifices, and the bride sees that her guests are sincere in their love for her. She knows the church is filled with family and friends she can rely on for support and strength in the future. God is glorified when we make a clear statement with the public witness of sincere worship.

Further, God is glorified by the life that is behind the love of his children. Just showing up for the wedding isn't enough. It isn't difficult to play the role of a loving and supportive family member for the brief time a wedding lasts, but will that love continue to be proven over time? Love is demonstrated by what you do day after difficult day. God is honored by the daily life his people live outside the church walls. I Peter 4:11 says, "Whoever speaks, is to do so as one who is speaking the utterances of God: whoever serves is to do so as one who is serving by the strength which God supplies; so that in all things God may be glorified through Jesus Christ, to whom belongs the glory and dominion forever and ever" (NASB). God is spirit and is made visible by the works of his people. Jesus said, "My father is glorified by this, that you bear much fruit, and so prove to be My disciples" (JOHN 15:8 NASB).

Finally, God glorifies himself. One way is through answered prayer: "And I will do whatever you ask in my name, so that the Son may bring glory to the Father" (JOHN 14:13). He glorifies himself by using his servants: "Israel, you are my servant. I will show my glory through you" (ISAIAH 49:3 NCV) Jesus was glorified through his birth, death, and resurrection, and will be glorified when he returns (JOHN 12:23). Each person of the Trinity focuses attention and gives honor to the others. The Father glorifies the Son: "If I glorify myself, my glory means nothing. My Father, whom you claim as your God, is the one who glorifies me (JOHN 8:54). The Son glorifies the Father: "The time has come. Glorify your Son, that your Son may glorify you" (JOHN 17:1). The Holy Spirit glorifies the Son: "When the Spirit of truth comes, he will guide you into all truth. . . . He will bring me glory" (JOHN 16:13–14 NLT).

HOW DOES WORSHIP RELATE TO THE OTHER PURPOSES OF OUR LIVES?

God is the One who made all things,
and all things are for his glory.
HEBREWS 2:10 NCV

*P*erhaps you are familiar with *The Purpose Driven Life*, written by my pastor and friend Rick Warren. In that book, Rick explains that God created us to live in a balance between the five biblical purposes found in the Great Commandment (LUKE 10:27) and the Great Commission (MATTHEW 28:19–20).

- In the Great Commandment, we're told to love the Lord with all our heart, soul, strength, and mind. This is the essence of worship.

- In the same passage, we're told to love our neighbor as if we're loving ourselves. This is the basis for ministry.

- The Great Commission commands us to go. This is our mandate for evangelism.

- In the same passage, we're told to make disciples. We're told to teach God's people to obey. This means we must disciple believers in the ways of God.

- Finally, we're also told to baptize in the name of Jesus, showing the world that these new believers now belong to the family of God. They not only believe; they also belong. This is the foundation for fellowship.

At Saddleback, we state the five purposes in this order: worship, fellowship, discipleship, service, and evangelism. But regardless of how the list is organized, all five purposes are equally important and vital to a spiritually healthy and well-balanced believer.

Yet it is important to understand the distinction between worship as a purpose and worship as a way of life. A life of worship is *how* we live, while the purpose of worship is one of the reasons *why* we live. This means that "worship" as a verb is expressed in all five of the biblical purposes, and it also means worship as a purpose is not limited to mere acts of worship like praying or singing.

First, as a believer, you worship when you fellowship; you worship when you grow spiritually; you worship when you serve others; and you worship when you tell others about your faith. It's all worship. Jesus prayed to God, "I brought glory to you here on earth by doing everything you told me to do" (John 17:4 nlt).

Further, you cannot honor God through the purpose of worship unless it is also balanced with the purposes of fellowship, discipleship, service, and evangelism. The five biblical purposes are interconnected and can only be experienced in concert with each other.

Jesus not only taught the five purposes; he kept them balanced in his life:

- *To Worship God*—He brought God pleasure: "This is My beloved Son, in whom I am well-pleased" (Matthew 3:17 nasb).

- *To Fellowship*—He loved the church and gave his life for it (EPHESIANS 5:25). He was baptized into the fellowship of God (MARK 1:9-11).

- *To Become Like Christ*—Because Jesus is Christ, he did not have to become like himself; however, the Bible says he studied and that he was found sitting in the temple, listening to the teachers and asking them questions (LUKE 2:46). It also says Jesus grew in wisdom and stature with God and men (LUKE 2:52). We need to do the same.

- *To Serve God*—Jesus served God and others. Regarding the works of Jesus, the Apostle John wrote, "If every one of them were written down, I suppose that even the whole world would not have room for the books that would be written" (JOHN 21:25).

- *To Witness to the World*—Jesus said, "I am the light of the world. Whoever follows me will never walk in darkness, but will have the light of life" (JOHN 8:12).

Finally, we begin our personal relationship with God through faith by grace. By faith we believe and we trust God with our life, surrendering our will to his. At the very core of worship is surrender. Worship is the foundation of how we live our lives. God's kindness leads us to repentance. It is through the surrender of our will that the Holy Spirit changes the course of our lives.

The soil of a worshiping heart is that which allows the seed of faith to grow and produce fruit. Rick Warren has taught me, "Surrender is not the best way to live; it is the only way to live." So we make it our goal to please God (2 CORINTHIANS 5:9).

> *A life of worship is how we live,*
> *while the purpose of worship is one of*
> *the reasons why we live.*

WHY IS LOVE FOR OTHER PEOPLE
IMPORTANT TO WORSHIP?

First, God commands us to not only love him, but also to love others. It is the second part of the Great Commandment: "Love your neighbor as yourself" (MATTHEW 22:40). Our love for other believers is so vital to our faith that Jesus said it is a mark of our discipleship; by loving other believers, we show the world that our hearts have been transformed by God (JOHN 13:35).

When you consider that worship requires you to take the focus off of yourself and aim it toward God, then you begin to see why loving others is foundational to a life of biblical worship. Authentic worship calls us to be others–centered instead of self–centered; we're to remove ourselves from the throne of our lives and put God there, where he's always belonged. In a sense, we are practicing for worship when we take our focus off of ourselves and begin to truly love the people around us.

Further, how can we successfully abandon self-centeredness and focus on God if we remain self-centered in our relationship with others? Jesus considered our relationships so important that he said, "If you are offering your gift at the altar and there remember that your brother has something against you, leave your gift there in front of the altar. First go and be reconciled to your brother; then come and offer your gift" (MATTHEW 5:23–24). Without love, even our worship can sound like "a noisy bell or a ringing cymbal" to God (1 CORINTHIANS 13:1 NCV).

Finally, love activates the fruit of the Spirit, such as joy, peace, patience, kindness, and faithfulness. The Apostle Paul says, "Against such things there is no law" (GALATIANS 5:22–23). As my friend Steve Pettit often teaches, these character qualities don't originate in you; they're not learned by study alone; and they can't be imitated by sheer willpower. They come from the one true God and appear only when we abandon ourselves to "the faith in the Son of God" (GALATIANS 2:20). Love *only* and love *always* brings us into an intimate, worshipful relationship with our Creator.

IS IT OKAY TO ENJOY WORSHIPING GOD?

I was glad when they said unto me,
let us go into the house of the LORD.
PSALM 122:1 KJV

There is a subtle but significant difference between enjoying the worship of God and merely enjoying the act of worship. The worship of God is not intended for the worshiper's enjoyment. An assembly that is primarily designed to be enjoyed by the participants is entertainment, not worship. God's Word predicts that, in the last days, selfish pleasure will take precedence over authentic worship: "They will be sneaky, reckless, and puffed up with pride. Instead of loving God, they will love pleasure" (2 TIMOTHY 3:4 CEV).

Going through the motions of worship for selfish reasons is foolish. Is God deceived by outward appearances? Has he lost his sense of smell? (ISAIAH 1:12) God knows whether we worship for his sake or our own because he looks into the heart of the worshiper.

David enjoyed worship and understood that God appreciated the heart and life of the "upright" worshiper. He wrote: "I know also, my God, that thou triest the heart, and hast pleasure in uprightness. As for me, in the uprightness of mine heart I have willingly offered all these things: and now have I seen with joy thy people, which are present here, to offer willingly unto thee" (1 CHRONICLES 29:17 KJV).

The fact that worship is primarily for God's benefit does not exclude the worshiper from deriving benefits from worship. Notice that David not only enjoyed worshiping but took joy in watching others worship, too. Enjoying worship is not only appropriate for the believer, it also is unavoidable!

Jesus was full of joy as he worshiped the Father: "At that time Jesus, full of joy through the Holy Spirit, said, "I praise you, Father, Lord of heaven and earth'" (LUKE 10:21). It is impossible to honestly celebrate and not enjoy it at the same time. Psalm 35:9 says, "Then my soul will rejoice in the LORD and delight in his salvation." According to the Bible, worship is joy–full!

First, enjoying worship is biblical. The phrase "rejoice in the Lord" is used forty–four times in the NIV Bible. Consider these verses, too:

- "Rejoice before the LORD your God" (LEVITICUS 23:40 KJV).

- "Glory ye in his holy name: let the heart of them rejoice that seek the LORD" (1 CHRONICLES 16:10 KJV).

- "I will be glad and rejoice in thee. I will sing praise to thy name, O thou most High" (PSALM 9:2 KJV).

- "Let all those that seek thee rejoice and be glad in thee let such as love thy salvation say continually, the LORD be magnified" (PSALM 40:16 KJV).

- "Let the righteous be glad; let them rejoice before God: let them exceedingly rejoice" (PSALM 68:3 KJV).

- "Rejoice in the Lord always. Again I will say, rejoice!" (PHILIPPIANS 4:4 NKJV).

- "Be glad in the LORD, and rejoice, O righteous, and shout for joy, all you upright in heart" (PSALM 32:11 ESV).

- "May my meditation be pleasing to him, for I rejoice in the LORD" (PSALM 104:34 ESV).

- "[Noah] consistently followed God's will and enjoyed a close relationship with him" (Genesis 6:9 nlt).

Further, it's natural to enjoy worshiping our life-changing, live-saving, and life-giving God! The Bible says, "For God so loved the world, that he gave his only begotten Son that whosoever believeth in him should not perish, but have everlasting life" (John 3:16 kjv). Just the thought of God's love for us— the greatest gift we will ever receive—should fill our hearts, souls, minds, and bodies with incredible joy!

The Bible also says, "You turned my wailing into dancing; you removed my sackcloth and clothed me with joy, that my heart may sing to you and not be silent. O Lord my God, I will give you thanks forever" (Psalm 30:11–12). There is no greater joy than the joy found in God. Worship is an appropriate response to who God is and what he has done. It's impossible for a believer to truly worship God without also enjoying the moment.

Finally, on a personal note, I enjoy worshiping God for several reasons:

1. I enjoy spending time with God. He fills my life with joy in his presence now and forever (PSALM 16:11, ACTS 2:28).

2. I enjoy watching, hearing, and joining others in worship. One of the most fulfilling aspects of my role as a worship leader is watching our congregation engage in worship. I enjoy hearing them sing, singing with them (not at them), and seeing the joy of the Lord revealed in their faces (PSALM 34:3).

3. I enjoy living a life of worship. Pastor Rick Warren says, "Your goal is not a feeling, but a continual awareness of the reality that God is always present. That is the lifestyle of worship."

4. I enjoy the ways worship changes my life (PSALM 34:4, PHILIPPIANS 1:6).

WHY DO WE LOVE WORSHIP?

*F*irst, it is important in answering this question to make the distinction between loving the act of worship and loving the God we worship. Our worship should always be for the benefit of God; we're to love our Creator and not merely the creative acts of worship.

Certainly, we're allowed to enjoy great worship experiences, but God should always be the focus of our worship. If the behavior of worship becomes the center of our worship, then we've moved into worshiping the work of our own hands (ISAIAH 2:8), and God calls this wicked (MARK 7:7). We do, no doubt, benefit from our worship of God, and even feel great joy as we worship, but the primary reason for worshiping God is not for our benefit; it is for God's pleasure as we express our gratitude and love for him.

Further, as we love God, our love for him will compel us to worship him. The more we understand who he is and what he has done for us, the greater our expression of love will be: "I was glad when they said unto me,

130

'Let us go into the house of the LORD' " (PSALM 122:1 KJV). "Surely goodness and mercy shall follow me all the days of my life and I will dwell in the house of the LORD forever" (PSALM 23:6 KJV; see also PSALM 40:8; 84:10).

C. S. Lewis says that as we understand the majesty and omnipotence of God, our expression of love for him will become as natural as the way we express amazement for an artist after looking at a great masterpiece.

Finally, God created us to seek him through worship. We want to fill the God–shaped hole deep inside each of us, and the only way to fill it is with God himself. When we worship, we're reminded anew of God's great love for us: "Within your temple, O God, we meditate on your unfailing love" (PSALM 48:9). As our hearts fill with love for God, worship allows us to express that which is ready to burst from within us: "You alone are the LORD. You made the heavens, even the highest heavens, and all their starry host, the earth and all that is on it, the seas and all that is in them. You give life to everything, and the multitudes of heaven worship you" (NEHEMIAH 9:6).

Responding to God in worship allows us to rejoice, celebrate, exult, be glad, and delight. The list is nearly endless; consider these additional verses related to how we can respond to God through worship.

Psalm 5:11

John 16:22

Habakkuk 3:18

1 Chronicles 16:10

Psalm 9:2

Psalm 89:16

Psalm 40:16

Philippians 4:4

Psalm 40:8

Psalm 35:27

Psalm 70:4

Revelation 19:7

Psalm 119:16

Psalm 16:11

Psalm 37:4

WHY ARE SOME PEOPLE AFRAID
TO WORSHIP GOD?

*I*t's hard to imagine why anyone would be afraid to worship. A loving relationship with God is the most wonderful and fulfilling experience a person could possibly have in this lifetime. "Nothing else compares with it" (PROVERBS 3:13 TLB).

Some people are afraid of the unknown. Some may be struggling with guilt or shame. Others may be afraid of the changes that worshiping God might make in their lives. But being afraid of worship is like being afraid of a baby. No one is afraid of the baby itself, but what might be intimidating are the sacrifices, commitments, time requirements, changes in priorities, and new things to learn. With a baby you must become open both to loving someone with more love than you ever thought you could give and someone loving you with a love you know you don't deserve. People might be afraid of worship because they don't believe unconditional love— from God or to God—is really possible.

Jesus had an assurance for those whose hearts are fearful of worship: "Peace I leave with you; my peace I give you. I do not give to you as the world gives. Do not let your hearts be troubled and do not be afraid" (JOHN 14:27).

Here are three reasons someone might be afraid to worship.

First, some people who say they are afraid to worship may actually fear the crowd in a worship assembly. The fear of crowds—called *ochlophobia*—can cause panic attacks and rob people of some of life's most priceless experiences. Some therapists direct patients to confront the fear by putting themselves in crowd situations. Other patients conquer their fear by regaining control of their emotions and retraining their subconscious minds.

Further, some people fear the consequences of attending worship services. Publicly associating with Christians can come at high personal cost to relationships, finances, or even personal safety. Some people might face serious pressure from family and friends who reject Christ. Others may face persecution from government or other religious leaders. Still others may have had negative experiences with a church or with a father figure; people who have suffered abuse at the hands of an earthly father may be afraid to trust their heavenly Father or even enter his house.

Finally, a sense of guilt can cause a natural fear of judgment. Have you ever felt the fear of taking a final exam you didn't study for? Genesis 3:10 says, "And He said, I heard thy voice in the garden, and I was afraid, because I was naked, and I hid myself" (KJV). Some people avoid God because they fear dealing with the consequences of their personal failures.

> *People whose eyes are riveted on themselves*
> *cannot focus upon God.*
> —GEORGE BARNA

Nº 28

WHAT ARE THE BENEFITS OF WORSHIPING GOD?

Every good and perfect gift is from above,
coming down from the Father of heavenly lights.

JAMES 1:17

First, the primary benefit of worshiping God is God himself! Worship is the first and greatest commandment, and it is required of all believers. "You may finally decide that you want to worship only the LORD. . . . No one has ever heard of another god even trying to do such things as the LORD your God has done for you" (DEUTERONOMY 4:29, 34 CEV).

"The LORD will be with you and help you, as long as you obey and worship him" (2 CHRONICLES 15:2 CEV). One way God shows us that he is on our side is through answering the requests of worshipers; he answers our prayers. "You can ask [God] for anything in my name, and I will do it, for this will bring praise to the Father because of what I, the Son, will do for you" (JOHN 14:13 TLB).

Further, God offers the worshiper the benefit of protection and joy while on earth and the promise of eternal life in heaven. "But make everyone rejoice who puts his trust in you. Keep them shouting for joy because you are defending them. Fill all who love you with your happiness. For you bless the godly man, O LORD; you protect him with your shield of love" (PSALM 5:11–12 TLB).

Not only are worshipers promised the joy of the Lord while on this earth; they're also promised the JOY that waits in heaven. Heaven will be the worship experience of all worship experiences, and Jesus said he is preparing a place for every believer. He's coming back to get us soon, so we can live with him! (JOHN 14:2, JOHN 10:27–28) "Eye has not seen, nor ear heard, nor have entered into the heart of man the things which God has prepared for those who love Him" (1 CORINTHIANS 2:9 NKJV).

Finally, every promise of God, written in the Bible, is a fantastic benefit to the worshiper. God's promises include:

A long life—DEUTERONOMY 6:2

God's mercy—ZEPHANIAH 2:3

Beholding the beauty of the Lord—PSALM 27:4

Joy—PSALM 16:11

Forgiveness—1 JOHN 1:9

Guidance—PSALM 25:12

Friendship with God—PSALM 25:14

Provision—MATTHEW 6:3

His grace is sufficient—2 CORINTHIANS 12:9

Help when tempted—1 CORINTHIANS 10:13; JUDE 24

Hope during hard times—ROMANS 8:28

"Praise the LORD, O my soul,

and forget not all his benefits."

PSALM 103:2

WORSHIP

With all my heart, soul, and strength for

Only the one true God in

Reverence

Service and

Humility

In everything I do, may

my life always bring

Pleasure to you.

CHRIST
of the
Upward WAY

Christ of the upward way, my Guide divine,

Where Thou hast set Thy feet, may I place mine;

And move and march wherever Thou hast trod,

Keeping face forward up the hill of God.

Give me the heart to hear Thy voice and will,

That without fault or fear I may fulfill

Thy purpose with a glad and holy zest,

Like one who would not bring less than his best.

Give me the eye to see each chance to serve,

Then send me strength to rise with steady nerve,

And leap at once with kind and helpful deed,

To the sure succor of a soul in need.

Words: Walter Mathams, c. 1915
Music: "Sursum Corda" (1834-1884)

Give me the good stout arm to shield the right,

And wield Thy sword of truth with all my might,

That, in the warfare I must wage for Thee,

More than a victor I may ever be.

Christ of the upward way, my Guide divine,

Where Thou hast set Thy feet, may I place mine;

And when Thy last call comes, serene and clear,

Calm may my answer be, "Lord, I am here."

Not fame, wealth, power, and other worldly ambitions.

   Not cleverness or great ability.

But purity of heart,

   clearness of vision,

      and singleness of purpose

   are the essentials.

HOW CAN WORSHIP CHANGE
SOMEONE'S LIFE?

*A*ll of us have something in us that compels us to worship, to put something on the throne of our lives. And we can count on the fact that whatever we choose to worship will have a dramatic impact on the quality of our lives, for better or worse. We are indeed wired for worship. We'll worship something. Somehow. The only question regards what we choose to worship. We might not worship God. Instead, we might worship people such as celebrities, athletes, cover models, or business moguls. Or we might worship alluring, intangible things like earthly wealth, or power, or fame, or outward beauty, or achievement, or even human sensuality. And whatever we choose to worship in this life—be it God or man, be it life giving or life stealing—the object of our devotion goes a long way toward determining the trajectory of the most important things in life: our relationships with other people and our relationship with the Creator.

First, a life dedicated to learning how to worship God will make us wise. The book of Proverbs promises that the "fear of the LORD is the beginning of wisdom" (9:10). This is not fear as in being cowed or shivering in a dark corner somewhere. This is a fear rooted in awe and respect and amazement. As we walk through life and come to a deeper understanding of who God is, our only response is one of awe. In awe of the amazing mystery and dimensions of a God who, since Day One, has done things for us because of a not–of–this–world brand of love for us. When we begin to realize the depth and sweep of this love, we begin to understand how to walk through this life in a better, more profound, more meaningful way. It makes us wiser about the full range of all the decisions and choices we make in this life. Worship leads to wisdom, and wisdom leads to a well–lived life. That's a promise we can clutch in confidence.

Further, worshiping God will help us during hard times. Throughout the Scriptures godly people face all manner of troubles and afflictions. That's a reality of life this side of Eden. The world doesn't work like it's supposed to. Not anymore. But these same God–seeking pilgrims in the Bible, because they understood who God is and what he's about—that he wants us to know how loved we truly are—they understood that God was, and still is, an absolutely reliable source of comfort and peace during seasons of pain and hardship and grief. They received this comfort and peace—a peace that defies human understanding (PHILIPPIANS 4:7)—because they worshiped God no matter what the circumstances of their lives. And they could worship God under any of life's circumstances, just as we can today, because a life dedicated to worshiping God is a life dedicated to a profound understanding of the source of all our freedom and security.

Finally, worshiping God helps set things right both in our individual lives and in the world at large. When the Creator of the world is being worshiped by his creation, all is right. Things get restored. Redemption and reconciliation happen. This occurs in the global sense as believers gather to be with one another in seeking God. But it also happens in the private life of a worship–bent individual who seeks God in weekly, daily, hourly, and even minute–by–minute encounters. Over time, a genuine God–seeking worshiper will put more and more of the important things in his or her life in the right place, in the right order, because that person's worship is in the right place. This will help each of us be better in all the roles we hold most dear. Better spouses, better parents, better friends, better sons, better daughters, better neighbors. It'll make us more giving, more gracious, more loving. In so doing, we'll be a part of helping to set things right. Ultimately, worshiping God will bring an unending joy into our lives—because, as the psalmist writes, God can turn "mourning into dancing" during hard times (PSALM 30:11), and, during the best of times, God can be the unequalled inspiration of our singing, dancing, and exaltation as we come to a better understanding of who God is and develop ever–grateful spirits.

HOW CAN I GET BEYOND THE IMPURITIES IN MY HEART TO WORSHIP GOD?

*I*t is important to remember how much God loves us. When he looks at you and me, he looks through his perfect Son, Jesus, and sees us as his children . . . clean, perfect by grace, and precious to him. Incredible!

The Bible says that "while we were yet sinners" (ROMANS 5:8–11) Christ died for us. We need to let go of our guilt. Paul says to forget the past and press on toward our future in Christ (PHILIPPIANS 3:13). Paul also urges us to offer our bodies as living sacrifices, holy and pleasing to God, as a spiritual act of worship (ROMANS 12:1). In becoming pure, we first offer our lives to God; our obedience is worship. Christ did the second part of making us holy and pleasing to God when he paid for our sins on the cross. Then Paul instructs us not to conform any longer to this world, but instead to be transformed by renewing our minds (ROMANS 12:2).

Many times when I am distracted while having a quiet time or worshiping the Lord, I will pause to write down the distraction or thought and then will resume my time with the Lord. I don't feel guilty about being distracted; I just stop and deal with it. Sometimes when I am leading worship and I feel down or troubled, I deliberately hand all my troubles over to the Lord as an act of faith and then worship through the storm. I believe this is authentic worship—coming to God just as we are in reverence, submission, and service. Remember, we come to God by grace through faith (EPHESIANS 2:8–10). None of us is righteous on our own (ROMANS 3:10).

A great way to keep impurities from invading your mind is to concentrate on pure things instead. Read Philippians 4:8 and James 1:22–25. Remember, God loves you!

Brothers, continue to think about the things that are good and worthy of praise. Think about the things that are true and honorable and right and pure and beautiful and respected.

PHILIPPIANS 4:8 NCV

*The truly happy people
are those who carefully study
God's perfect law that makes people free,
and they continue to study it.
They do not forget what they heard,
but they obey what God's teaching says.
Those who do this will be made happy.*

JAMES 1:25 NCV

HOW CAN I GET BEYOND THE SELF-CONDEMNATION THAT ATTACKS MY MIND?

This is not an uncommon problem. At some point, each of us has felt or done something that a follower of Christ shouldn't do. The devil reminds us of our weak moments to accuse us, telling us we're not sincere, driving a wedge into our worship relationship with God.

The shield of faith protects us from the enemy's fiery arrows (EPHESIANS 6:16). If it came down to feelings or behavior, no one could enter God's presence. No one deserves God's grace. "All have sinned and fall short of the glory of God" (ROMANS 3:23). "There is none righteous, no, not one" (ROMANS 3:10 NKJV).

Faith is trusting God to keep his promise to "forgive us our sins and to cleanse us from *all* unrighteousness" (1 JOHN 1:9 NKJV, emphasis added). Faith is trusting in the fact that God loves us—a fact that does not change because of our hurts, habits, or hang-ups. Rejoice in the mystery of God's grace!

A quick survey of the people of the Bible clearly demonstrates that imperfection does not prevent God from using us—and should not keep us from worshiping him. Adam, Noah, Abraham, Moses, David, Peter, Paul—all were human and all were sinners, but God's strength is made perfect in weakness (2 CORINTHIANS 12:9). Our imperfections and failures even become an avenue for God's grace to work: "God causes everything to work together for the good of those who love God and are called according to his purpose for them" (ROMANS 8:28 NLT).

Here are three things to remember the next time self-condemnation tries to distract you from worship.

First, even Jesus' closest followers struggled with fear and doubt. They were firsthand witnesses to his amazing life, yet they were still frightened sometimes. Jesus told them, "Peace be with you" (JOHN 20:19). When Thomas doubted the exciting stories that Jesus was in fact alive, Jesus reassured him: "Don't be upset, and don't let all these doubting questions take over. Look at my hands, look at my feet. It's really me. Touch me.

Look me over from head to toe" (JOHN 20:27 PARAPHRASE).
It seemed too good to be true. When it seems too good
to be true that God loves you, remember that you are
completely loved, forgiven, and acceptable to God by
grace through faith—period! While we were still
sinners, God loved us (ROMANS 5:8), and his love will
never end (PSALM 136).

Further, even if you never get past the attacks on
your mind, you still can choose to ignore them. Take
those thoughts captive and make them obedient to
Christ (2 CORINTHIANS 10:5). Fill your mind with
Scripture—reading and memorizing—so God's Word
can replace your self-condemnation. Ask God to point
out anything in your life that displeases him, and then
allow his forgiveness to wipe it away: "Search me,
O God, and know my heart: try me, and know my
thoughts: and see if there be any wicked way in me, and
lead me in the way everlasting (PSALM 139:23–24 KJV).

Finally, let go of the past and look to the future
God has in store for you. "Forgetting what is behind
and straining toward what is ahead, I press on toward

the goal to win the prize for which God has called me heavenward in Christ Jesus" (PHILIPPIANS 3:13–14).

Keep focused on the mission God has given you. "The most important thing is that I complete my mission. I want to finish the work that the Lord Jesus gave me—to tell people the Good News about God's grace" (ACTS 20:24 NCV).

When self–condemnation undermines your confidence in Christ and threatens to prevent your worship, remember that your sin debt is paid in full. "There is no condemnation for those who belong to Christ Jesus" (ROMANS 8:1 NLT). Celebrate and savor your freedom in Christ. "Make sure that you stay free, and don't get tied up again in slavery to the law" (GAL. 5:1 NLT).

Jesus knows your heart better than you do, and he loves you . . . he loves you . . . he loves you!

HOW CAN WE WORSHIP
WHEN LIFE IS HARD?

This challenging concept is easiest to grasp when we remind ourselves that the singlemost important desire God has for us is that we each become, over time, a truly loving person. In fact, if we had to boil down the whole message of the Bible into one sentence, that's what it would be—that God wants us to spend ourselves in a quest to become extravagant lovers of him and others. The path to that beautiful outcome is often crossed by life's stream of difficulties, but learning to deal graciously with adversity teaches us so much. This reminds me of a simple, profound poem called "Along the Road" written by Robert Browning Hamilton.

> I walked a mile with Pleasure;
> She chattered all the way;
> But left me none the wiser
> For all she had to say.

I walked a mile with Sorrow;

And ne'er a word said she;

But oh! The things I learned from her

When Sorrow walked with me that day.

So we can worship—which is giving God all that we can with all that we are—in hard times, because we can be confident that God wants the best for us, and we understand that all which comes our way in this life can help shape us into more loving people. In time, we can understand this axiom so deeply that we can strive to do what James urges us: "Consider it pure joy, my brothers, whenever you face trials of many kinds, because you know that the testing of your faith develops perseverance. Perseverance must finish its work so that you may be mature and complete, not lacking anything" (JAMES 1:2–4).

First, hardship and suffering are part of life this side of Eden, and it does not surprise God when pain strikes us. We live in a fallen world. Jesus knew this. He told us how to prepare for tough times, such as when thieves break in and steal our stuff (MATTHEW 6:19). Not "if," but "when." Jesus knew the nature of human existence would mean that the things we hold most dear would be subject to all manner of bandits. This includes both earthly treasures and also intangible things we value, such as joy and peace. Not only did Jesus know this, he experienced it firsthand. At the end of his life Jesus suffered deep agony. He acknowledged this in the account of the Last Supper (LUKE 22:28) when he told the disciples, "You are those who have stood by me in my trials." We can take great comfort in the fact that Jesus himself has gone before us by suffering so much, in the quest to fulfill an act of love the world has yet to fully understand.

Further, God is near us in times of trouble (ISAIAH 57:15), maybe even nearer then than during good times. This is not because God moves away from us during the good times, but because we often move away from him. It's a truism that when things are going well for us we often become less dedicated and less passionate about staying close to God through prayer, reading his Word, and living a contemplative life. But when life brings us grief or pain or discouragement, we learn how God uses the "bread of adversity" and the "water of affliction" (Isaiah 30:20) to grow our faith, increase our wisdom, and expand our capacity to love.

Finally, we often want answers and explanations during seasons of turmoil, which is understandable, but God gives us something far more profound—relationship. Nowhere is this transformational truth more evident than in the Old Testament account of the story of Job. After Job had lost nearly everything dear to him, he came to realize that God was there all the time, listening to Job's loudest prayers and to his quietest sobs. Everyone around him, including his wife, had told Job to curse God for what had happened. Job asked God time and again why he had to endure so much pain and anguish. He wanted answers. And what Job learned is that God, the Creator of the universe, understood his pain and ached for him. In the end, Job was changed because he came to understand a startling thing about the nature of God: God loved him deeply and was there with him. Today, God so much wants to be close to each one of us. What happened between God and Job is a beautiful example of what we most have to offer others who are going through life's hard times—our presence, compassion, and empathy. When we truly understand the dimensions of what's happening when we face life's challenges, when we realize how much God cares and how high his hopes for us are, we can worship wholeheartedly even in times of hurting.

> *Is the ambient noise level of my life*
> *low enough for me to hear*
> *the whispers of the Lord?*
> –BILL HYBELS

MUSIC...
and More

Rejoice in the LORD, O you righteous!
For praise from the upright is beautiful.
Praise the LORD with the harp;
Make melody to Him with an instrument of ten strings.
Sing to Him a new song;
Play skillfully with a shout of joy.

PSALM 33:1-3 NKJV

Worship is so much more than music, yet music remains a key element to our worship of God. Music often breaks through our defenses that words cannot overcome, and it helps calm our spirits as we approach the Throne of Grace.

WHAT IS MUSIC'S ROLE IN WORSHIP?

*"Love the LORD your God with all your heart and with all your
soul and with all your mind and with all your strength."*

MARK 12:30

Music itself is not worship; it's a language of worship.
It's a way we express our love for God. For example,
when we worship, God speaks to us through the lyrics
and the music's profound simplicity, grandeur, and
beauty. Aristotle once said, "Music has the power to
shape character." As a musician I wholeheartedly agree.

God created this powerful medium for his purposes.
Throughout the ages it has been an important part of
helping churches reach their communities and help
people grow into spiritual maturity. The music style
that a church uses in its services will greatly impact who
that church will reach.

Let's look at the role of music in Christian worship.
Music uses every facet of our human nature—heart,
soul, mind, and strength—to help us as we worship.

First, music communicates directly to our hearts and souls. It is an international language every heart understands. It often can express what is in our heart like nothing else. By connecting to our souls—who we really are as individuals and as children of God—music helps us tell God what we can't say with mere words.

Further, there is an underappreciated mental aspect to music as well. Music is a great way to teach theology. It helps our minds organize and recall information. People remember songs much easier than sermons. As Pastor Rick says, "A song can often touch people in a way that a sermon can't." Using music to teach spiritual truth is a biblical idea. Colossians 3:16 says, "Let the word of Christ dwell in you richly in all wisdom; *teaching* and *admonishing* one another *in psalms and hymns and spiritual songs*, singing with grace in your hearts to the Lord" (KJV, EMPHASIS ADDED). At Saddleback, Pastor Rick and I use a teaching format that I call "Point and Play": when the pastor makes a point in his message, the music team reinforces it by playing a song that matches that point. This has been an effective way to tell a story at Saddleback.

Finally, when people sing or play musical instruments they engage their strength in worship. The physical act of making music has spiritual impact (1 SAMUEL 16:16; PSALM 57:7-9). I'm not sure how music created from flesh and bones can communicate on a spiritual level, but it does. And very well at that.

God created music for his pleasure. When we use music to give him thanks (PSALM 92:1), to celebrate what he has done in our lives (PSALM 100:2), or to declare his faithfulness (PSALM 92:2), we are using music as an act of worship fit for the King we serve. Music may not be worship in itself, but it's a powerful love language to our heavenly Father.

> *When we face up to the Glory of God,*
> *we soon find ourselves*
> *face down in worship.*
> –MATT REDMAN

WHAT MAKES MUSIC SACRED OR SECULAR?

What makes music sacred or secular is how it is used.

The Bible is the inerrant Word of God, so in the strictest sense, the only Christian music or sacred songs are Scripture songs—either psalms or songs directly quoting Scripture. No musical notes are included in the Bible, probably because the precise tune and style are not of eternal consequence. Although the ministry of the musician is recognized in Scripture, the truth is in the lyrics, not the music.

With that in mind, let's define a sacred song today simply as "any song that can be used in church." This includes instrumental-only songs that are powerfully used to communicate about God and worship him.

Lyrics indicate the message of a song, and although many songs don't have a message appropriate for use in the church environment, there are plenty of others that can be used to help direct the congregation's attention to God. By examining the content of a song, most people can tell whether or not it is appropriate. A song doesn't necessarily need to be excluded based solely on the artist who wrote or recorded it.

In the same way that nature can be used to point to God, an otherwise secular song can be sacred if it's used for the purposes of God. Music is a gift from God and was intended to be used for his purposes. On the surface, a flower is just a pretty thing to put in a vase, a sunset is just the sun going down, and the beach is just a place where the water meets the land; but God can touch our hearts with the beauty and fragrance of that flower, the intricacy of his creation exemplified by that sunset, or by the immense power and vast size of the ocean. Similarly, God can use secular songs to reach us with profound spiritual implications because he is the ultimate source of everything good (JAMES 1:17). He put the talent in the songwriter, and he put the God–shaped hole in each of us. Whether or not a songwriter has acknowledged that hole and let God fill his or her life is irrelevant in terms of the spiritual usefulness of a song. At Saddleback, we've seen God use many secular songs with profound spiritual messages—such as Peter Gabriel's "In Your Eyes," Lou Graham's "I Want To Know What Love Is" or songs from U2 and Sister Hazel—to touch people during our worship services.

Something ordinary can become sacred when used for God's purposes. For instance, Moses, one of the greatest leaders mentioned in the Bible, used a common staff as he guided flocks of sheep until one day when God took that staff to use it for his own purposes (EXODUS 4). From that day forward the secular staff became a sacred staff.

Things are sacred or secular based on their use in light of God's design. God is the only true Creator. He redeems that which is secular and makes it sacred according to his purposes, even you and me. I once was lost, but now I am found. . . . Praise God!

WHAT MAKES A SONG A WORSHIP SONG?

*P*astor Rick Warren says there's no such thing as Christian music. I would add that there is no such thing as non–Christian music. Music style is more about culture than about theology. Our culture tends to define music by its style, the combination of instruments resulting in some recognizable category of sound. We talk about styles such as jazz, rock, classical, country, Tejano, and more. However, there isn't a sound or style that is specifically Christian music. Instead, Christian and Gospel music come in a wide variety of music styles. Worship is simply one purpose of music, and it is defined based on the message of the music, not the style.

The message is what makes a worship song a worship song. Worship is our response to what, or in our case who, we value most. A song can be a tool of worship to bring the truth of God, God's Word, from our head into our spirit. Any song that helps people devote more of their lives to God is a worship song. The goal of worship is to lead people to respond to the greatness of the one and only living God. "Therefore, I urge you, brothers, in view of God's mercy, to offer your bodies as living sacrifices, holy and pleasing to God—this is your spiritual (reasonable) act of worship" (ROMANS 12:1).

Of course, there are different types of worship songs. In our services at Saddleback, we use a basic model for worship flow in order to lead people into an intimate place with God. It's called the IMPACT model:

Inspire

Movement

Praise

Adoration

Commitment

Tie it Together

All of these types of songs are worship songs based on their lyrics, but they serve different specific purposes as part of the general purpose to INSPIRE worship.

People don't necessarily arrive at church already in worship, though, so we warm up with hand–clapping songs that inspire MOVEMENT. PRAISE songs are hand–clapping songs about God's character and deeds. ADORATION songs are hand–joining songs about how we feel about who God is and what he has done. COMMITMENT songs are hand–raising songs that offer our personal response to God. TIE IT TOGETHER songs are hand–joining songs of fellowship that affirm we are part of God's family. This general model is a way to help remember our goal.

So what makes a song a worship song? Any song— when it has a message used for God's purposes—is a worship song.

Worship songs must communicate Christ. If your audience doesn't understand the language of old hymns, use them less often.

Ultimately, there are many different styles of worship music because there are many different types of people. In some ways, just the fact that we talk about "classic" hymns or "contemporary" songs betrays the

influence of our own culture bias. The great hymns of
our faith today were often considered much too
worldly/contemporary in their own time, just as many
of the contemporary songs of today will become
"classic hymns" in the future of the Church. Imagine if
a Jewish believer of Jesus' time were to attend even the
most traditional church of our modern day. He'd hear
nothing familiar in the music itself, but his spirit could
resonate with those believers' spirits through worship.

Worship music communicates biblical doctrine and
helps to change lives. The purpose of the worship service
is not music education or music preservation but life
transformation. Worship leaders must present worship to
an Audience of One while leading an audience to be won.

HOW LOUD IS TOO LOUD?

*T*here is no disputing that the Scripture speaks of loud worship: "Sing unto him a new song; play skillfully with a loud noise" (PSALM 33:3 KJV). "All the Levites who were musicians . . . [played] cymbals, harps and lyres. They were accompanied by 120 priests sounding trumpets" (2 CHRONICLES 5:12). A musical reference even is used to describe a loud noise in heaven: "And I heard a voice from heaven, like the sound of many waters and like the sound of loud thunder, and the voice which I heard was like the sound of harpists playing on their harps" (REVELATION 14:2 NASB).

This question, however, is about *too* loud, not just loud. While loud is biblical and can be useful, too loud is neither. How do we know when the music is too loud? ("Huh?" "Whadya say?" "I can't hear you!")

First, the music is too loud when the volume distracts from worship. Years ago I attended a wonderful worship event that featured incredible singing. I had never heard people sing so loudly! Hearing other people sing encouraged others to sing, and the spirit of worship rose. At one point, however, the organist opened up with a showy demonstration of the power of the pipe organ. The music was so loud it actually covered all the voices! In that moment, my focus shifted from the music to the musician. I stopped singing and started watching the organist. While many people there showed great appreciation for the exhibition, I felt like we exchanged an opportunity to worship for an instrumental demonstration. The volume of the music is just right when it is not noticed. Our bodies should feel the music, not notice the volume.

Further, the music is too loud when it is no longer musical. High volume is not a synonym for excellence. Beginning musicians often try to use loud volume to make up for a lack of accuracy and practice—as if the louder they play, the better their musicianship will sound. And the higher volume sometimes causes the individual musicians to turn up their own instruments in a desperate effort to hear themselves play. This leads to diminished clarity and tone quality of the instruments and less musicality. A better solution is to turn down sounds that mask others. For example, if a guitar player needs more volume, asking the drummer to play softer may be a better solution than amping up the guitar. Dynamics—varying the volume—also is an essential part of communicating with music. When the music is only one volume, whether loud or soft, it becomes less musical and has less impact. Using dynamics is a great way to improve communication.

Finally, the music is too loud when it causes hearing loss. Repeated exposure to loud noise can cause permanent damage and hearing loss. If people need to shout to be heard above the music, then the volume is too loud. A typical conversation is about 60 decibels. Exposure to noise levels at 85 decibels or higher for more than eight hours a day puts your hearing at risk, although a noise that ranks lower on the decibel scale but that continues for longer periods of time actually may be more harmful to your hearing than is an intermittent, higher intensity noise. At my church we use a decibel meter at the soundboard to monitor the volume. The volume limit is 96 decibels, similar to that of a hand drill, spray painter, or bulldozer—and much softer than a chain saw (110 decibels), an ambulance siren (120 decibels), or a rock concert (130–140 decibels).

It would take continuous exposure to sounds at 100 decibels—such as a very loud worship band and an energetic teacher with a microphone—for about one to two hours, the average length of a church service, to cause permanent hearing loss. Church musicians are at more risk than the rest of the congregation because they are closer to the sound and are exposed to the volume longer. It's never too late to do what you can to protect your hearing. Always have earplugs handy (usually the more expensive models are better), and use discretion with volume.

HOW CAN MUSIC IN WEDDINGS AND FUNERALS BE WORSHIPFUL?

*F*unerals and weddings are often many people's first exposure to the church's ministry, and these types of services deserve the best preparation we can offer, musically and in prayer.

Based on the family's needs and desires, the pastor should minister in an appropriate manner, both in speaking and in music. Those of us who officiate need to remember our first priority is to serve the Lord, then serve the family and their guests. The speaker has the responsibility to present the truth of God's Word clearly through these services that present opportunities for people's hearts to be wide open to the Gospel.

Not every song a family suggests should be used in the funeral or wedding. However, when at all possible, it is my preference to honor the family's song suggestions.

Many "generic" love songs can be appropriate for a Christian wedding. God obviously enjoys the

love–marriage relationship because it was his idea.
Wedding songs can celebrate love without specifically
mentioning the Creator of love.

When I agree to serve at a funeral or wedding,
I consult with the family and ask if they have songs in
mind. I get a general sense of their musical style
preferences and where the family is spiritually, and then I
suggest songs that will minister to the family at their level.

The opportunities for worship at a funeral are as
unique as the person who has died. For instance, there's
a huge difference between the loss of someone who
died of old age having served their church faithfully
and having raised a family of believers and that of a
teenager who died in a freak accident. The needs of
the mourners are very different. Always consider the
audience. Resist the temptation to rely on a generic
solution; the music and speaking need to fit the specific
families. Use a variety of hymns, songs, and
contemporary worship songs that speak of hope, grace,
the promise of eternity, and comfort.

CAN WE WORSHIP WITHOUT
SINGING OR TALKING?

*S*inging and speaking are marvelous ways to participate in worship, but some believers relate better to God in other ways. *God is much more interested in the heart from which we worship then he is in the art form with which we worship.*

The human heart is able to express worship in many ways that transcend verbal communication. Isaiah 52:15 says, "Kings will be silent as they bow in wonder. They will see and think about things they have never seen or thought about before" (CEV). God enjoys authentic worship expressed through the entire diversity of personalities, culture, methods, and styles that he himself created.

Although worship does not require speaking or singing, worship does require action of some kind. For example, God says, "Be still and know that I am God" (PSALM 46:10). That requires action in at least two ways: (1) obedience as we stop moving, and (2) focusing our attention and thoughts on God. Knowing God, in turn, causes other action—he changes the way we think and that affects the way we live our lives.

So what are some ways believers can worship without involving singing or speaking?

First, we can express worship through physical acts—bowing, kneeling, lifting hands, creating art, and dancing are examples of biblical worship expressions (EXODUS 31:2-14; 2 SAMUEL 6:14; 1 KINGS, 8:54; 2 CHRONICLES 7:3; PSALM 45:1; PSALM 95:6; PSALM 149:3; ACTS 21:5). Service and work also can be acts of worship because as Jesus explained, "When you did it to the least of these, my brothers and sisters, you were doing it to me" (MATTHEW 25:40 NLT). Every believer should view work and daily life as opportunities to worship.

Further, all five senses—hearing, sight, taste, touch, and smell—can be used to worship God. Each one of these senses was created to be used for God's glory. Worshiping with all five senses is similar to watching a movie with surround sound rather than a mono speaker. God gave us five speakers, if you will, to bring us the richest experiences of him possible this side of heaven. For more on the five senses, see pages 70-73 of this book.

Finally, we can worship through silent prayer and meditation. There is a time to be silent and a time to speak (ECCLESIASTES 3:7). Prayer needs to precede, saturate, and follow all worship expressions, as the Bible instructs us to pray without ceasing (1 THESSALONIANS 5:17). Silent prayer is a wonderful way to worship. And although it seems silent to us, we can be sure it echoes loudly in heaven! Here are a few examples of silent prayer and meditation from God's Word:

> Hannah prayed silently—1 SAMUEL 1:12–15
>
> Be silent in God's presence—HABAKKUK 2:20, ZECHARIAH 2:13
>
> Meditate on God's word—JOSHUA 1:8
>
> Meditate on God's love—PSALM 48:9
>
> Meditate on God's works—PSALM 77:12

Take a moment right now to worship God through silent prayer and meditation!

WHERE DID THE DANCING GO?

Scripture shows us that dance played a significant role in joyous celebration among God's people. Exodus 15:20 tells us that Miriam, Aaron's sister, led all the women of Israel "in rhythm and dance" after God delivered the Hebrews from Pharaoh's army at the Red Sea. King David danced vigorously "before the Lord" to celebrate the arrival of the Ark of the Covenant at Jerusalem (2 SAMUEL 6:14). Through the prophet Jeremiah, the Lord promised his people would "dance merrily" when he restored them from captivity (JEREMIAH 31:4).

Even the glum old Preacher of Ecclesiastes acknowledged there is a time to dance! (ECCLESIASTES 3:4)

In most churches today, however, you never see dancing. What happened? Is dance one of those things, like animal sacrifices, that Christians don't have to do? Why don't more churches use dance in their worship services? Are we not joyful enough to dance? Is dancing unscriptural?

First, as an expression of worship, dancing is as biblical as any of today's commonly used worship methods—including singing and teaching. "Let them praise his name in the dance: let them sing praises unto him with the timbrel and harp" (PSALM 149:3 KJV). Music, dancing, and singing were ingrained in the culture of Israel. Dance was a natural and appropriate expression of joyous worship. Don't you think it remarkable that the Hebrews—former slaves fleeing Egypt for their lives, not knowing where they were going or how long they would be traveling—thought to bring their tambourines? Lots of tambourines! These people must have danced often when they worshiped and celebrated!

However, a common problem with dancing in the church today is that, like any art form, our culture associates it with entertainment. A lot of "church dance" actually turns out anything but entertaining. If a church includes dance in a worship service, but then that dancing is not well prepared or skillfully presented, the church will be less likely use dance again in the future. Poor dancing draws the worshipers' attention away from worship. Like poor singing, poor dancing makes people uncomfortable. And like singing, not everyone who likes to dance should be dancing in front of a crowd! When done well, dance speaks to the soul in ways that other forms of communication cannot. But dance in the context of a worship service must be done thoughtfully, skillfully, and appropriately. This requires a qualified director, talented dancers, adequate rehearsals, and a workable rehearsal space. Dance in the church must not be anything less than excellent.

Finally, some churches associate dancing with sensuality. Paul said, "Whether you eat or drink or whatever you do, do it all for the glory of God. Do not cause anyone to stumble, whether Jews, Greeks or the church of God" (1 CORINTHIANS 10:31–32). The concern about stumbling is valid, of course, but it must not be allowed to excuse ignoring a powerful art form that enriches worship. Sermons and committee meetings can also cause people to stumble, but most churches still include those! Dancing is no different from any other expression of worship in that it must be done in a proper and orderly way. "My friends, when you meet to worship, you must do everything for the good of everyone there" (1 CORINTHIANS 14:26 CEV). "Do everything properly and in order" (1 CORINTHIANS 14:40 CEV).

I hope more churches will open their arms to the appropriate expression of dance in worship. I admire the attitude of many dancers who have been patiently waiting for years to use their gifts at church, adopting as their motto the selfless words of Paul: "For I am not seeking my own good but the good of many, so that they may be saved" (1 CORINTHIANS 10:33).

> *Anything you do*
> *that brings pleasure to God*
> *is an act of worship.*
> –RICK WARREN

IS IT WORSHIP WHEN WE GIVE
MONEY TO THE CHURCH?

*G*iving can be a difficult topic, and it has been widely misinterpreted by some people. But Jesus talked more about giving than about heaven, hell, or even prayer. Just read through the Gospels and see how often he refers to the state of our heart being directly related to our desire to give—our time, energy, empathy, and material possessions—so that widows, orphans, the sick, the homeless, and others in distress can be helped.

Being a follower of Jesus definitely means being a giver. Giving to the church is a way for us to worship God, because whenever we do something to thank God or praise him or glorify him, it's an act of worship. We can worship God with our bodies when we sing or pray. We can worship God with our minds by meditating on the Scriptures and earnestly seeking out God's ways. And we can worship God with our possessions when we joyfully give to the church to help meet the needs of others. Each of us "should give what he has decided in his heart to give, not reluctantly or under compulsion, for God loves a cheerful giver" (2 CORINTHIANS 9:7). Giving because you think you have to, or out of a legalistic obligation, is not really giving. God's vision for us in this area is so much grander and life affirming.

First, the New Testament has numerous passages that describe a stunning picture of the giving and generosity God yearns for in the church and in our own lives. In the early church, believers gave because they chose to. They had experienced God's generosity in their own lives and they wanted to pass it on. When they passed it on—and when we, in our generation, pass on what's been given to us—God's light and goodness is brought to a shadow–filled world. Acts 4:32 says believers didn't think of possessions as their own, and they sold them to meet the needs of others. They didn't have to do this; they wanted to. In 2 Corinthians 8:2–4, the Apostle Paul stood amazed at the Macedonian churches, which gave so much even though they themselves were in great distress. "Out of the most severe trial," Paul writes, "their overflowing joy and their extreme poverty welled up in rich generosity."

They gave out of a deep, profound response to what God had done for them. This is the very essence of worship, our coming to grips with who God is and who we are, and our responding in joy and gratitude. We become generous givers because we realize that God has given so much. It's not out of fear or a sense of duty. It's a way for us to love God, love others, and understand our part in making the world a better place.

Further, it's the job of the church to help others both with spiritual needs and also with physical, everyday needs. And this can't happen without money and resources. When we give to the church, we are helping accomplish what God expects from us as believers. God's hope for us is that we are radically generous when spontaneous life needs come up for others, like with the Good Samaritan. And also that we joyfully embrace giving to and investing in things that'll last for eternity, which is to be the unique, chief activity of the church. Jesus implores us in Matthew 6:19–21: "Do not store up for yourselves treasures on earth, where moth and rust destroy, and where thieves break in and steal. But store up for yourselves treasures in heaven, where moth and rust do not destroy, and where thieves do not break in and steal. For where your treasure is, there your heart will be also." The mission of the church—to spread the Gospel and, more importantly, to *be* the Gospel—can be the most valuable thing that happens on earth in terms of the impact it can have on people's lives and our world. And in the wisdom and incalculable imagination and genius of our Creator, that cannot happen without the hearts of believers being moved and committed to contributing out of the money and possessions we've been given.

Finally, any wise believer will tell you the priceless irony that ultimately the person who probably most benefits from a generous, giving heart is the giver himself or herself. This is often the way it is with a God whose ways are not ours. You cannot become a cheerful, lavish, unselfish giver without experiencing invaluable spiritual growth that makes you more Christlike. This is the very passion of a true disciple of Jesus and very much the desire of God for each of us.

As we become more and more generous, we become living, breathing expressions of God's grace to others. This spreading of God's grace will not only repel the money—focused forces pressing on our lives and in the world at large—greed, materialism, consumerism, exploitation, self—indulgence—but it will yield peace, joy, freedom, contentment, all of the attributes of a truly abundant, well—lived life.

GROUP
WORSHIP

May my friends sing and shout for joy.
May they always say, "Praise the greatness of the Lord.
He loves to see his servants do well."
I will tell of your goodness.
I will praise you every day.

PSALM 35:27-28 NCV

God never intended for Christians to walk out our faith alone; we're meant to live in Christian community. The same is true of worship: we may be compelled to worship God alone, and we can treasure those private moments with him. However, God also designed us to worship together, collectively lifting our voices of praise to him and sending a sweet aroma to his throne.

WHY DOES GOD WANT US TO
BELONG TO A CHURCH?

The Bible says the church is an incredibly special thing. In fact, the church is described in the Scriptures as the "bride" of Christ. That's a powerful and compelling metaphor for where the church stands in God's eyes. The church's mission is no less compelling: to be the ultimate model of love to the world, the outward expression of God's incomparable passion for people everywhere. The church demonstrates this not–of–this–world brand of love by showing uncommon compassion and unity, and by making a difference in people's lives. And here's the real kicker: the church is not a building. It's us. You and me. It's people. Where we meet is unimportant. That we meet is of utmost importance. Why? Because the church's overall purpose— being the delivery system of God's redeeming love to a love–parched world—is so essential to the fulfillment of potential in our lives individually, and to the plight of every generation.

First, though, let's acknowledge that you can follow Jesus without even ever having a conversation with another believer. Some of our brothers and sisters, in fact, have no choice but to carry out their Christian walks this way. Some people are infirm and can't get to a church. Others may be imprisoned. Others may live in isolated places. And others dwell in parts of the world where church is illegal. So it can be done. It's just very difficult to do. And it's not at all ideal. And it's not what God desires. We can know this based on the many, many passages about the nature of the church in the New Testament. The book of Hebrews warns against "forsaking the assembly." There's just so much you miss out on by not seeking out and gathering with other believers learning to do what Jesus called us to do— love God and others better and better, deeper and deeper, year after year.

Further, the Greek word for *church* means "an assembly" or "gathering of people." In the Gospels and in the book of Acts, we see people gathering and meeting together all the time in the first-century church. Acts 20:7 refers to the practice of the early believers coming together to "break bread" and to hear the Apostle Paul's preaching. There are references to believers praising God together. If you think about it, certain things crucial to a believer's life can only really happen in a community of other believers. For instance, every believer has spiritual gifts from God (1 Corinthians 12). God intends for those gifts to be used for the common good of you and me and the others around us so that we can mature in our relationships with God and with one another. The books of 1 Thessalonians, James, and Hebrews are filled with "one anothers" that believers fulfill when they assemble: comfort one another; build up one another; confess sin to one another; pray for one another; and "spur one another on toward love and good deeds."

Finally, Jesus promised that whenever and wherever two or more believers would gather, his spirit would be present. And whenever Jesus' spirit is present, any and every good thing we can imagine is possible.

WHAT DOES UNITY HAVE TO DO
WITH WORSHIP?

If you bear in mind the true end of worship and the beautiful dream Jesus has for us—the reconciliation one day of God and all God's children with him and with one another—you'll understand why a spirit of unity is so essential to a life of worship. Worship is a beautiful, mysterious, life–altering thing, but even worship is not an end in itself. God desires our honest, humble, unified worship, but not because the Creator of all there is and ever has been needs anything from us. God wants our hearts to be in the right place with him and with one another as part of worship, because that is the path to restoration of all God cares most deeply about. Over and over again in the Scriptures, the unity of believers in true, God–pleasing worship emerges—from the earliest references to worship in the Old Testament, to Jesus' comment that the Pharisees' worship was a farce because their hearts were distant from God and from others, to the descriptions of all humanity worshiping God at the end of human history. There's no mistaking it: God knows the profound role unity plays in bringing healing and wholeness. And this unspeakable, near–unfathomable harmony is the desire of God. Just think about what God has already done, through Jesus, to draw near to us. God wants unity for us and with us, maybe even more than we want it for ourselves sometimes.

To achieve unity in worship, first leave your offering and go get right with your brother or sister. It isn't necessarily easy to understand that trying to get right with God requires us to try to get right with one another, but it is simple . . . and true. Even the fallen Jewish king, Saul, understood this; Saul, in 1 Samuel 15, confessed his sinful nature to the prophet Samuel, and he asked for Samuel's forgiveness so he could then go worship the Lord. Genuine worship involves sacrifice and humility. And it takes a sacrifice on our part sometimes to put unity before our own thoughts and feelings. We need to do all we can to be right with those God has put in our sphere of relationships before we can have a chance to be right with our Creator. This is true whether it's an individual believer and his circle of family and friends, or an individual body of believers with one another, or the global body of Christ.

Further, when we act for the sake of unity, we are acting according to an uncommon, others–oriented love. And when we tap into that kind of selfless love, and we make it more important than issues or opinions, we are embracing the very Spirit of God and joining the Spirit in his work of reaching others who don't yet know Jesus and of growing believers in their faith. This work makes possible the most improbable, most majestic of scenes—"all humanity will come to worship" (ISAIAH 66) and "I will give them one heart and mind to worship" (JEREMIAH 32).

Finally, without the Spirit we cannot have worship that is pleasing to God. Psalm 5 says that if we're truly on the path to understanding God, we will enter the temple "with deepest awe." Let's face it: we cannot possibly be in a state of awe of the Creator if we're holding onto harmful, painful, division–causing things against a part of his Creation, especially somebody in

God's family or our own. Jesus emphasized this so strongly in Matthew 15 when he said of the Pharisees and religious scholars, "Their worship is a farce, for they replace God's commands with their own man—made teachings." And what are the greatest two commands of the God of the universe? Love God. Love others. Everything else is a distant third. The Pharisees' worship was false, Jesus said, because their hearts were "far away." There was neither love nor unity.

Where there is unity, there is love. Where there is love, there is God. Where there is God, there is the Spirit. And where there is Spirit, there is the potential for every good thing. Which is the very thing God has had in mind for us since the beginning of days.

Patience and encouragement come from God. And I pray that God will help you all agree with each other the way Christ Jesus wants. Then you will all be joined together, and you will give glory to God the Father of our Lord Jesus Christ.
ROMANS 15:5-6 NCV

HOW CAN I MOVE BEYOND MY AWARENESS OF PEOPLE AROUND ME AND REALLY LET MYSELF GO INTO AN INTIMATE PLACE WITH THE LORD?

We can define "an intimate place with the Lord" in as many ways as there are different personalities.

Consider the examples of David and Jesus.

David was intimate with God and was known as a man after God's own heart, but he also was an outgoing, creative type who enjoyed a good party (1 SAMUEL 13:14). David danced before the Lord with great abandon (2 SAMUEL 6:14). When he was criticized he responded by declaring, "In God's presence I'll dance all I want!" (2 SAMUEL 6:21 MSG). Then he said, "I'll dance to God's glory more recklessly even than this. And as far as I'm concerned . . . I'll gladly look like a fool" (2 SAMUEL 6:22 MSG).

No one was more intimate with God than Jesus, and he often retreated from the crowds to be alone with God (LUKE 5:16).

God created us all with different personalities. Authentic worship requires integrity. Just being who God created you to be pleases him.

Some of us are shouters or have demonstrative personalities. Some of us worship most fervently amid peace and quiet. God enjoys variety of expression, and he is worthy of it all.

In worship, we need to focus on what God thinks about us, not on what we feel people are thinking about us. One way we can do this is through loving service. When we serve—which is worship—we shift the focus from our needs to others' needs.

Here are a few ideas to help us all experience intimacy with the Lord in a group setting:

- If we feel like people are watching us, we can simply move toward the back of the room where not as many people will notice us.

- We can try to see others as a part of the experience rather than a distraction. Don't try to block out those around you. One of the benefits of corporate worship is the sense of unity and family.

- Sometimes when leading worship I will stop singing and listen to the congregation sing. Listening to others worship God can be an intimate, beautiful experience.

- And remember, although distractions can interfere with worship, personal sin is the greatest threat to intimacy with God (GENESIS 2:25). If you can't get into worship, examine your own spirit.

> *The reason why many are still troubled,*
> *still seeking, still making little forward progress*
> *is because they haven't yet come*
> *to the end of themselves. We're still trying*
> *to give orders, and interfering with*
> *God's work within us.*
>
> –A. W. TOZER

FALL ON ME

Holy Spirit fall

Fall on me

Holy Spirit fall

Fall on me

On my hands

On my feet

On my heart

Every part of me

Fall

Spirit of peace

Sent by the Father's hand

Change my life with Your presence

Make me whole

Pour over me

Like rain on a thirsty land

Make a stream in the desert

Of my soul

—RICK MUCHOW

WHAT KIND OF PARTICIPATIVE WORSHIP IS APPROPRIATE FOR AN EVANGELISTIC, SEEKER-SENSITIVE SERVICE?

For a seeker-sensitive worship service in a large group, I would do no more than fifteen minutes of congregational singing plus two specials. If the group is small then I would do less congregational singing and more performance. The total service time, including preaching, for an evangelistic service shouldn't be longer than an hour. If the worship service is primarily an assembly for believers, then I would expand to thirty minutes of congregational singing.

The larger a congregation is, the more you can sing. Smaller groups often make singing awkward, because it's possible that only a few people will know all the songs. In an evangelistic setting, songs must be understood by everyone. Nonbelievers can certainly watch worship—it is a testimony to them—but they cannot truly worship.

An example of an understandable song for a nonbeliever is "How Great Is Our God." This is a deep song that is seeker sensitive without diluting the Gospel. Nonbelievers can understand the language of this song.

I love hymns, but in seeker–sensitive services many of our cherished hymns don't work. Some hymns use language that's at least two hundred years old, and even some contemporary songs are written in such Christianese that nonbelievers can't understand them. Phrases like "lift him up," "power of your blood," "wash me in your blood," "cleanse me in your fire," "blood of the Lamb," "exalt your name," or "anointed Word" are tough for nonbelievers to understand. Many great songs need a lot of explanation to be used effectively in an evangelistic setting. Also, avoid songs that require vocal gymnastics. If the song is not easily singable, then you've created another communication hurdle with a seeker–oriented audience as they concentrate on how to sing the song rather than focusing on what the song means.

The goal in any worship service is for people to connect with God in spirit and in truth. Seeker–sensitive services are often tilted toward praise (about God's attributes) rather than to worship (our response to who God is).

The seeker–sensitive service is simply a user–friendly event based on the language used to connect those people to God in a way they can understand. A seeker–sensitive service can be any kind of worship gathering. It's not about less power or depth or compromising the Gospel; it's about who can understand. I think of seeker–sensitive services as having people over to my house for the first time. We'll probably relax in the living room, family room or maybe the kitchen, but we won't hang out in the bedroom. My wife will ask in advance what our guests like to eat, and she'll prepare a quality meal based on their preferences. That's the way we'll start to grow new relationships.

LEADING
and
MANAGING
WORSHIP

> "The people must build a holy place for me. Then I can live among them. Build this Holy Tent and everything in it by the plan I will show you."
>
> EXODUS 25:8-9 NCV

God loves worship of all kinds, and I'm confident he's well pleased when we break into spontaneous worship. But, if you're a worship leader, then part of your role is to help create an atmosphere of worship that guides your congregation into intimate moments with the Heavenly Father. The answers in this section will benefit anyone seeking to develop greater skills as a worship leader—even if you're simply leading yourself in worship. (For more Q&As on leading and managing worship, visit my website at www.encouragingmusic.com.)

WHAT ARE KEY POINTS OF LEADING A VIBRANT WORSHIP MINISTRY?

Vibrant worship is a lot more than an enthusiastic crowd enjoying an intimate atmosphere and singing songs with a great worship band. Worship involves nothing less than offering up our whole lives to God so that all we do is in conformity with God's character and standards rather than with the attitudes and values of the world (ROMANS 12:1–2).

In addition, the vast majority of the world's cultures love and respond to music. Music is by far the most influential art form of the day. Worship is not creative art, nor is it the art of public speaking. Worship starts with a believer's attitude toward and focus on God. Worship is an expression of our love and thanksgiving to God. Without that perspective, our "worship" can often become just singing or even mere entertainment. Just coming to church and singing a few songs is not where worship starts. The effective worship leader understands that worship leading is not just leading songs; it's leading lives to life change.

Here are tips for effective worship L.E.A.D.I.N.G.:

Let God lead

Engage the senior pastor's philosophy of ministry

Align with the other purposes of the church

Define your target

Inspire by example

Never stop loving those you are leading

Give your best

Let God lead

Jesus said that he is the vine and that we are the branches. Apart from him we can do nothing (John 15:5). Being effective musically does not guarantee effective corporate worship. In my experience, God is more interested in the heart than the art. Pastor Rick Warren taught me years ago that the local church belongs to God and that it is only by his grace that he uses us. Our leadership and the congregation's participation both start with focusing on God.

ENGAGE THE SENIOR PASTOR'S PHILOSOPHY OF MINISTRY

There are many methods and styles of ministry. As long as they are effective and do not violate Scripture, they are valid. There are many different kinds of churches because there are many different kinds of personalities and cultures. In most cases the worship leader of a church is not the primary leader of the church and, therefore, does not set the philosophy of ministry for the church. My role at Saddleback is to support the senior pastor's philosophy of ministry through worship. Before I came on staff, the most important thing that my pastor wanted to know was not about my talent, professional background, or personality, but whether or not we shared the same biblical doctrine and if I embraced his strategy, style, and ministry methods.

ALIGN WITH THE OTHER PURPOSES OF THE CHURCH

The Great Commission and the Great Commandment outline five purposes of the church—Magnification (Worship), Membership (Fellowship),

Maturity (Discipleship), Ministry, and Missions (Evangelism). Along with the five purposes of the church there must be a defined purpose for each event or service. For example, a Bible study might be intended to grow people in maturity, and worship could be incorporated to support that purpose. On the other hand, a missions-oriented event might need an entirely different approach in worship. Working with clear objectives for each event eliminates guesswork and helps leaders prepare more effectively.

DEFINE YOUR TARGET

Know whom you are going to reach. In worship leading, the most important reason to identify your target is culture and language. For example, an unchurched person does not understand the church culture and its language, but profound spiritual concepts can be communicated in simple ways that fit the language and culture of the target audience. This means that the lyrics, musical style, and presentation must be appropriate for the target's maturity level.

INSPIRE BY EXAMPLE—BE THE LEAD WORSHIPER

The most important thing that every worship leader must do is love the Lord with all their heart, mind, and soul. Excellent programming, artistry, and production cannot replace the power of God released through a genuine and contrite heart. During rehearsal and sound check it is appropriate to be both pastor and producer/director, but when leading worship . . . worship! Refuse to produce while worshiping. If the drummer is dragging or something "wrong" is going on, try to coach your team without needing to have your own way. Don't look for mistakes as if the band is being tested but give your best to God. As you sing "I Love You, Lord," say it directly to God, not to the audience. People respond to sincerity and will follow its example.

NEVER STOP LOVING THOSE YOU ARE LEADING

The second part of the Great Commandment is to love your neighbor as yourself. What happens when we are criticized or feel unappreciated or the crowd doesn't feel like participating? Sometimes the natural thing to do is to get frustrated or angry. Everyone has an opinion about music, so what about when people rate your performance? Remember that Jesus loved us from the cross. We should be able to take some criticism and still love people. Remember that God often uses critics to teach us something about ourselves as well cause us to evaluate and improve our ministry skills. Stick with the fundamentals: Love the Lord with all your heart, mind, and soul, and love your neighbor as yourself.

GIVE YOUR BEST

1. One of the most important things a worship leader can do is be prepared.

2. Memorize your music and the order of service.

3. Prepare your team (musically, emotionally, and spiritually).

4. Be spiritually ready, physically fit, and emotionally rested yourself.

5. Have the appropriate equipment in place and in working order.

6. Plan ahead as much as possible.

Other tips for giving your best:

- Delegate: Let others take on some tasks so you can serve out of your strengths (EPHESIANS 4:7–16).

- Avoid comparing yourself and your team to the latest professional worship recording.

- Learn by listening, but don't compare.

- Evaluate for excellence. It is important to get feedback from your team and the congregation, especially from people who will tell you the truth, not just give you compliments.

- Keep growing musically.

- Keep the song set fresh by introducing new songs.

- Avoid the pitfalls of temptation (EPHESIANS 5:1–21).

HOW SHOULD SOMEONE PREPARE
TO BE A WORSHIP LEADER?

This is a great question, but another question needs to be asked first: "Can that person do anything else with their life, or must they be a worship leader?" It's a question of S.H.A.P.E.—Spiritual Gifts, Heart, Abilities, Personality, Experiences. Only the last four of these can be developed; a worship leader must already possess the spiritual gift of prophecy/exhortation.

Leaders are learners. As soon as leaders stop learning, they have, in effect, stopped leading. A worship leader needs to consistently study worship, pursue experiences in leading worship, and, most of all, be a devoted worshiper.

Some churches have secondary worship services that offer good opportunities to learn. In one sense, that's what I did as I was learning. I learned as I led.

Also, in an internship with a church someone can learn in two years what they might otherwise pick up by trial and error over ten years.

Many resources deal with both the theology and the practice of worship. This list offers a few suggestions:

YOUR LOCAL COMMUNITY

Attend other churches and local worship events to observe and examine how worship is done.

MAGAZINES

Worship! Magazine (www.worshipmag.com)

Worship Leader (www.worshipleader.com)

Christian Musician (www.christianmusician.com)

BOOKS

Heart of the Artist by Rory Noland (www.willowcreek.com)

Unquenchable Worshiper by Matt Redman
(www.regalbooks.com)

The Air I Breathe by Louie Giglio
(www.multnomahbooks.com)

The Purpose Driven Church and *The Purpose Driven Life*
by Rick Warren (www.purposedriven.com)

The Way of a Worshipper by Buddy Owens
(www.purposedriven.com)

CONFERENCES

Purpose Driven Worship Conference
(www.purposedriven.com)

Passion (www.passionnow.org)

Christian Musician Summit
(www.christianmusiciansummit.com)

Soul Survivor (www.soulsurvivor.com)

Worship Together (www.worshiptogether.com)

ONLINE SEMINARY CLASSES

Liberty University (www.liberty.edu)

Dallas Baptist University (www.dbu.edu)

Rockbridge Seminary (www.rockbridgeseminary.com)

A worship leader starts from their S.H.A.P.E. and through consistent pursuit and commitment develops a personal life of increasing depth of worship from which they are able to lead and model worship for the body of Christ.

If someone loves the church and has a gift and calling for worship, there must be a place for him or her to serve. What a gift!

I try to include as many young people as possible in leading worship. My own children (all five of them) help me keep in touch with trends, and my desire is to keep worship relevant with our community's culture. The pastor of the church where I became a Christian must have taken a huge risk in inviting me and other youth to participate on the platform by singing in the choir, doing the sound, playing in the band, and the like. The music was different and we looked different. But at that time the church experienced vibrant growth as all ages worshiped together. As a congregation, we grew to embrace a unity of worship within our diversity. It was a truly inspiring and impacting time for me, and it helped lead me more deeply into the ministry serving where I am today. Growing up at that church, I felt valued, and because of that, I participated and brought my friends to church, as well.

WHAT IF YOUR SPIRIT IS DOWN WHEN YOU'RE SUPPOSED TO LEAD WORSHIP?

I'm passionate about this topic. This simple question is so profound, and it hits on a common need for all of us who lead worship.

Lead from your pain. Lead from your low point. Worship is our response to what we value the most or, in our case, who we value most. God shouts to us in our pain. The key is to rest our spirits in God's hands.

Surrender is one of the purist forms of worship. When going through pain or discouragement, if you will surrender those feelings and thoughts to God, you will be able to lead worship in an authentic way that perhaps in times of joy you would not be able to replicate. This can be difficult, but it will lead to deep intimacy that we as leaders can share with our congregation as we unite in worship.

Psalm 30:10–12 says, "Hear, O LORD, and be merciful to me; O LORD, be my help. You turned my wailing into dancing; you removed my sackcloth and clothed me with joy, that my heart may sing to you and not be silent. O LORD my God, I will give you thanks forever." That's what surrender brings. That process is our promise, and with this hope, we minister and worship from our weakness.

Here are some practical tips:

1. Ask God to be your strength before you greet your team or your congregation.

2. Realize that your intuition is obscured because of how you feel.

3. Use your emotions as you affirm this statement of faith: "We are hard pressed on every side, but not crushed; perplexed, but not in despair; persecuted, but not abandoned; struck down, but not destroyed. We always carry around in our body the death of Jesus, so that the life of Jesus may also be revealed in our body" (2 CORINTHIANS 4:8-11).

4. Go to your friends and family for support, prayer, and encouragement.

I have led from a position of weakness more times than from a position of strength. I've never been let down by God when I've trusted in him. He's always come through. It helps me to remember that it's not about me, it's about him.

TRUST GOD

Trust God from the bottom of your heart
Don't try to figure out everything on your own
Trust God for where your life is going
God is in control, God is in control

> *Commit to the Lord, whatever you do*
> *and your plans will succeed*
> *Pray, "Lord I'm available to you*
> *Here I am, Lord, use me"*

God is in control, God is in control
Trust God, trust God
Trust God, trust God, trust God

—Rick Muchow

Nº 48

WHAT ARE THE BASICS OF GETTING MY OWN MUSIC PUBLISHED?

God has blessed many worship leaders with the ability both to serve our specific church congregations and also to reach beyond our congregations through some of the songs we write.

I often write songs out of necessity. Songwriting has never been something I have done for an outside audience or specifically as a business effort. My approach as a worship leader has always been to seek out songs for the pastor's particular message—whether it's a specific theme or energy level or seeker sensitivity or whatever—and I have often found it easier to write a new song than to find an appropriate outside song. Then, sometimes, these songs are given a life outside of my local congregation.

Rather than focus on the process of getting signed to a record deal, I'm going to offer a big-picture look at the publishing aspects of songwriting.

The publishing business basically has three components: exploitation, protection, and song inventory. *Exploitation* is the industry term for letting others know about your songs. The term sounds negative, but it basically means getting exposure for your songs through various methods, including use on a CD, in a songbook, musical recordings, in films, and on television. *Protection* has to do with securing and administering copyrights and licensing fees/royalties. *Song inventory* is simply a publisher's portfolio of songs.

A publishing company is a business. Generally, song royalties are split 50/50 between a publisher and a songwriter, though that is certainly negotiable on both sides. Publishers make money by getting others to use the songs they represent, and success is very much about finding the right song in the right place at the right time.

As you pursue having your songs published, know that rejection is a part of the process. Rejection does not necessarily mean your song is bad, although it can. Most of the time, however, rejection means a song does not fill a need (style, product, vibe) for that publisher at that time.

Successful songwriters have working relationships with artists and publishers. Unsolicited submissions to artists or publishers will probably not get heard. It can happen, but just sending out demos is the least effective method of getting the right attention.

If you believe that your songs might benefit other worshipers, start with a small circle of connections and worship leaders, and then grow your exposure from there. You can venture forth through:

1) SONGWRITING OR MUSIC COMPETITIONS

Locate and figure out which competitions you want to pursue. Some resources include SongWriting.net (www.songwriting.net) and the John Lennon Song Writing Competition (www.jlsc.com).

2) MUSIC CONFERENCES AND FESTIVALS

Conferences and festivals take place around the country throughout the year. At Saddleback Church, we are relatively close to MUSICalifornia (www.musicalifornia.com), Spirit West Coast (www.spiritwestcoast.org), and The Christian Guitarists Conference (www.heartfeltmusic.org). I also would like to invite you to join Saddleback Church's annual Worship Conference and Festival, which features a Song Seeker component (www.purposedriven.com).

3) WORSHIP OR MUSIC MAGAZINES AND INTERNET SITES

Magazines and websites like *Worship Leader* (www.worshipleader.com), *Christian Musician* (www.christianmusician.com), and www.ShareSong.org often provide information for and about independent artists and songwriters, as well as indie–friendly ad space and free resource opportunities.

4) MUSIC OR DENOMINATIONAL ASSOCIATIONS

Look for music associations or denominational associations to which you can become a member and attend events.

5) LOCAL BENEFITS OR LIVE PERFORMANCES

Perform locally and regionally. You never know who

might hear your music and what opportunities might result. The experience, exposure, and fun can be great.

YOUR RELATIONSHIP NETWORK WITH ARTISTS & PUBLISHERS

Ultimately all of the above combine to create a relationship network for you. The placement of my song "The Greatest Mystery" in the film and on the soundtrack for *Left Behind II* was a direct result of the relationship network I had developed through thirteen years of ministry and songwriting. Connecting with the companies and artists who will use your songs starts and ends with the personal relationships you build. Those relationships are the best way to get heard.

ADMINISTRATION

On the administrative side of the business, you can use a service to protect (copyright) and administer your accounting for song royalties.

For every song, there are two options: self-publishing the song or assigning it to one or more publishers.

With self–publishing, you maintain control over the song, collect the full royalty, and have absolute freedom to do what you would like with the song. You can choose at any time whether the song is treated as a ministry product or as a business product. Sounds great, doesn't it! Of course, the flip side is that you alone are unlikely to have the connections and resources to get the song widely used or distributed.

On the other hand, you can assign the song to one or more publishers. This brings great connections and resources and frees you up from handling the business side of music. This also sounds great! Of course, the flip side here is that you have to give up control over your song, take a smaller cut of the royalties (although hopefully there will be more royalties), and you might be a small fish in their huge pond. The song then becomes a business product.

Here's illustration from my own experience that shows how these two approaches can differ. The scenario: a ministry would like to include one of my songs in their songbook. If that song is self–published,

I can make my own deal with the ministry about royalties (including the option of waiving all royalties and fees as a gift to the ministry), and I can immediately grant permission for the song to be included. If I have assigned that song to a publisher, I can tell the publisher that I want my song in the book—I can even waive my portion of the royalties—but ultimately the publisher decides what price the ministry must pay to include my song in their songbook. It is unlikely that a publisher would waive their own royalties entirely, because they have a business to run and expenses to cover.

OWNERSHIP

There are many possible answers to the question of who owns the music you write. Basically, though, if your job description includes writing songs, then it's likely that the songs belong to the church, whereas if your job description does not include writing songs, then you probably own the music you write.

HOW DO YOU DISCERN WHICH SONGS AND WHAT TYPES OF MUSIC YOUR CONGREGATION LONGS TO HEAR?

Song choice is a very important decision and can also be very difficult.

Always put the purposes before the personal preferences of the people. It's not about what kind of music our members want to hear but rather the most effective way to support and communicate the purpose of the service.

Here are some tips:

1. Support the theme of the message.
2. Match your music with your target audience. What kind of music do they like best?
3. Know your pastor's philosophy of ministry, and choose music that supports it.
4. Choose music that fits the singer.
5. Use words understandable to your audience.
6. When planning a seeker–sensitive worship

service, don't select songs simply because they are popular in the church culture.

7. Vary the tempos and style to keep interest.

8. Choose songs that are singable for the congregation.

9. Avoid extreme vocal ranges.

10. Add one new song a week or mix up the selections to keep your presentation fresh.

When finally selecting the style of music that is going to be used during a service, two thoughts must be kept in mind: 1) the songs chosen—both lyrically and stylistically—should relax nonbelievers, not intimidate them; and 2) the worship music should inspire church members to invite their nonchurched friends to a service.

HOW MUCH SHOULD A LEADER TALK DURING A WORSHIP SERVICE?

*T*he words we speak as we lead the congregation are just as important as the songs we sing. They need to be well planned. Announcements, song introductions, prayers, and other moments of speaking should be discussed before the worship service so they are concise, strategic, and effective.

When I lead the weekend services, I am free to speak whenever I want and for as long as I want, although obviously we have a service schedule and timeline. If I feel led, I am free to speak. My pastor also feels the freedom to ask me to talk less when he feels I am talking too much. We work together to balance each service.

I have found this axiom useful: "Let the singers sing and the speakers speak." God has given us all unique gifts to serve him. We should allow others to use their gifts and we should use ours.

Instead of only preparing the music, I recommend that worship leaders rehearse everything, including the prayer and introductions. Very few worship leaders make up songs by the Spirit's leading while in front of their congregation, and so it should also be with the words we speak as we lead.

Spirit–led does not mean unprepared. The Bible says, "Preach the Word; be *prepared* in season and out of season; correct, rebuke and encourage—with great patience and careful instruction" (2 TIMOTHY 4:2, EMPHASIS ADDED). "Prepared" implies that we have worked, studied, meditated, experienced. We're to have a plan, then be open to making changes. Spirit–led is not making things up as we go along. It is allowing God to take what we've prepared and bless it. It's being ready to scrap what we've planned if what we've planned isn't needed. It is allowing God to use what we've prepared however he wants to use it.

When I lead worship, the process speaks for me through the way I lead the songs, the songs I've selected, the words of encouragement, and more. All of these help me quickly connect the congregation to the presence of God, and then to fade into the background. I've found that brief, clear words of encouragement are generally enough, though at times I also feel led to say and do more. Remember, the Holy Spirit leads both on the platform and also during the planning of the service.

My planned speaking generally consists of a friendly welcome, encouragement to participate in the singing, direction to sit and stand, congregational prayer, and when necessary, crowd control to make room for more people. Very rarely will I use speaking to introduce a song. A good song explains itself.

In the end, people generally don't remember sermons and similar information for long. Instead, people remember sermons best when they are seen or sung. They can remember the truth found in the lyrics for a lifetime. Choose your songs wisely, present them well, and you will have more impact on your congregation than you could ever have by speaking.

WHO MAY PLAY IN THE BAND OR SING IN THE CHOIR?

Choir and band members at Saddleback are required to audition, uphold the witness of the church in their private lives, punctually attend weekly rehearsals, memorize all music, complete all of the church's Christian life and service seminars, regularly attend worship services, support the fellowship and unity of the ministry, and perform at all weekend services at least once a month.

But does everyone who plays in the band have to attend the church or at least be a Christian? No.

The choir or band ministry can be a great way to get nonbelievers involved in the church. Through the years, I have seen several musicians accept Christ after playing in the band. There is room for ministry inside the band, not just through the band. This is considered a delicate issue, but I see room for nonbelievers if you have open slots. You should always utilize the talent

God has provided in your church body first, but if there are open slots then there is potential for ministry.

So why wouldn't we want a nonbeliever to help lead worship, though? There are some great reasons:

1) Nonbelievers can't truly worship. (See page 38.) They don't know God, even though God is the one who provided their musical talent.

2) Nonbeliever might be mistaken for role models. Are band members seen as spiritual models because they are on the platform? Yes, but consider this: People often mistakenly assume that *everyone* they see at church is a Christian role model. Remember that we're all on a journey at various stages of maturity in faith.

It is important that the people on the platform uphold the general values of the church off the platform. They can't be living with their girlfriends/boyfriends. They can't be cheating people. They must have good reputations and generally good character. Most of us realize that merely being a Christian does not make us a good person. We are not better than nonbelievers, only forgiven.

I wouldn't utilize nonbelievers as leaders, but their talents can certainly be used. The musicians' talents come from the Lord, whether they know it or not, and their talents can bless your team and your congregation. I also wouldn't use a nonbeliever just to make the band or choir sound better. Use nonbelievers to fill roles that you can't fill within the congregation. You should always utilize the talent God has provided in your church body first, but if he's left open slots, then there is potential for ministry. Pray that the nonbelieving musicians who perform with you will become part of the congregation in the future!

What do you do with talented players who don't read music? First, thank God for them! A lot of churches would love to have professional players. At Saddleback, we write chord charts with rhythm notation for the band. Players who can't read are encouraged to try to follow the charts. It is amazing how they learn to read the charts with practice.

EVERY DAY

Every day, Lord
Help us to remember that
You love us
You love us

Every day, Lord
Help us to remember that
You love us

We believe in you
We belong to your family
And we're becoming more like you
All because of your love

—Rick Muchow

CHANGE
and
CONFLICT
in
WORSHIP

God is God, and we are not—that's why we worship him, but it also means we imperfect humans may find ourselves in conflict amid or surrounding worship. It may not be combative conflict; rather it may revolve around the anxiety of change. These next few pages will help you with a few of the common issues. (You can find other answers related to this topic at www.encouragingmusic.com.)

We worship God through his Spirit, and our pride is in Christ Jesus. We do not put trust in ourselves or anything we can do . . . I was so enthusiastic I tried to hurt the church. No one could find fault with the way I obeyed the law of Moses. Those things were important to me, but now I think they are worth nothing because of Christ. Not only those things, but I think that all things are worth nothing compared with the greatness of knowing Christ Jesus my Lord.

PHILIPPIANS 3:3, 6-8 NCV

WHAT IS THE FUTURE OF WORSHIP IN THE CHURCH?

*T*he future of worship is extremely bright, because one day God's will is going to be done "on earth as it is in heaven" (MATTHEW 6:10). The future is difficult to predict, but we can be sure that worship practices will continue to change—as they always have—and that God perfects our worship as we draw closer to "Kingdom come."

The Apostle Paul said King David served God in his own generation (ACTS 13:36). That speaks not only of his age group but also of the culture, technology, and global awareness available while David was alive. He used the tools and methods of his day to do God's work. While our theology of worship must never change, our worship methodology will change—must change—to adapt to the times in which we live.

Change in worship practice, however, is a touchy subject for many Christians. Today's debates about changes in worship are more about methodology than theology, but some Christians are convinced that new worship trends are the work of the devil. Yes, the volume might be increasing at your church, but it is most likely not Satan's work. And if it is the devil's work, we know it is a temporary condition. Jesus said, "I will build my church, and the gates of hell shall not prevail against it" (MATTHEW 16:18 KJV).

While the distant future of worship is difficult to predict, I believe the near future of worship will bear three distinctives in frequency of change, variety of venues, and emphasis on worship's role in life.

First, methods and styles will change even more rapidly in the near future. Change is hardly new, but the pace of change today is astonishing. Rather than resisting change in corporate worship practices, I encourage you to embrace it. The only permanent thing in life is change. We don't embrace change for the sake of change, but developments in culture, technology, and global awareness guarantee change will need to happen.

Further, churches will offer diverse worship styles and multiple service times and create additional "venues" instead of constructing larger buildings. Saddleback has twenty-three different worship venues (and increasing). Generations in the church will be connected through service more than through corporate worship experience. Personal worship preferences will be addressed in the same church. Rather than searching for a church with a different worship style, individual Christians will "search" within their own congregations for the worship style that relates personally to them.

Finally, the church will increasingly emphasize the connection between what is experienced at church and how it should change the way we live. Sermons and songs will continue to be important expressions of worship; however, other forms of communication—including dancing, drama, fine art, and technology—will be integrated, with storytelling through video leading the way.

HOW CAN WE MAKE THE TRANSITION FROM A TRADITIONAL WORSHIP SERVICE TO A MORE CONTEMPORARY ONE?

First, be sure that your congregation wants to grow in this way. How do you know they want this? My heart goes out to church members who are being alienated from their congregations because of music style or preference. Where are they supposed to go to church? Before your congregation can grow and work to fulfill the Great Commission, it must align itself with a philosophy and lifestyle of ministry. Once you're on the same philosophical page, how worship is done won't matter as much because your goals, not traditions, will be the focus. Then you can take the next step: determining the methods for growing and changing.

Remember, as you attempt this type of transition, seek God's will and not your own; love him with all your heart rather than loving your own goals; love your church as Christ loved his. And be committed to staying even if things get rough.

I have four major concerns when looking at the pace of transition: motivation, honor, productivity, and time frame.

MOTIVATION

We want our churches to transition so they are culturally relevant. We want to reach the younger generation, the future of our church, while also taking care not to be consumed by worldly messages about being young and hip.

We should check our motivation. Do we want to grow and maintain a healthy, balanced church body? Is our motivation in line with the purposes of the church? Remember, all churches share the same biblical purposes, but they have unique personalities.

Change must be accompanied by commitment from leadership to stay through the change. Just because someone else is successful doing something, doesn't make it right for your church. The worship pastor's motivation must be to serve and fulfill the senior pastor's philosophy of ministry. In practical terms, the senior pastor is responsible for choosing the style of music, while the worship pastor's role is to help interpret and support the senior pastor's philosophy of ministry for effectiveness in the service.

Transitioning an established service takes a lot more work and patience than just starting a brand-new service. I recommend that before you try changing a service, you might want to consider adding a "venue." A venue is a church service with the same message as the main service, but with a different music style for worship. At Saddleback, we have our classic service in the main worship center, a gospel venue, an overdrive (rock) venue, an acoustic venue (intimate worship with a younger feel), two singles venues (one older, one younger), and even an island music venue.

Can most churches offer a variety of venues? That depends on your worship team and resources. If you think you can't offer multiple venues due to lack of resources, then you should plan a carefully crafted blended service.

For transitioning to blended, contemporary worship, I first would speed up the slow, traditional songs.

Add some guitars and a vocal team to stand in front of your choir as well. Going from choir and organ directly to guitars, drums, and bass could send your current members into shock.

It's also important to consider the relevancy of the preaching style when looking at the overall feel of the service. A contemporary service needs to have a contemporary message and delivery as well as appropriate music. Additionally, your music must always match your target audience, which may or may not be the same demographic as those in your current congregation.

A carefully crafted, blended service is one where it is tough to tell an overall style, and there is something for everyone. A blended service is one in which nobody notices when the style of music is changing. Just as a commercial airplane needs to make course adjustments to reach its destination, a church can make significant changes with gradual consistent change. Airplane passengers are not concerned about turning; they just don't want to get tossed around the cabin. A carefully crafted, blended service allows a broad reach. One example might be simply including younger people on the platform to help engage younger audience members.

HONOR

Are we honoring our veteran believers in our worship services? My fear is that many of our longtime faithful are not being honored as the integral and necessary parts of the church body they are. Being older, should they be less involved or viewed as less valuable to the ministry of the church? The biblical command is to love our neighbors as ourselves. Don't let a musical style interfere with the love.

Just as we honor our older faithful, we also should honor our younger believers with their ideas and expressions of faith. I don't believe it is God's will for part of his body to meet in one place and part in another, never meeting together. With multiple venues, one of the ways the body can be brought together is through ministry and service. Although we may not all be able to sing together all of the time, we can always serve together.

PRODUCTIVITY

Making changes in an established congregation is generally done only for the health of the church. The church is the body of Christ. Just like our own physical body, the church body needs to grow, adapt to change, and take care of itself. Some mature churches may realize they haven't "worked out" in a long time. It hurts to go back into the gym, so to speak. It takes discipline and commitment, but it's important to be in good spiritual shape so we can do our best for God.

People who haven't exercised in quite a while are always advised to see a physician. This applies to churches, too. A carefully planned program designed to fit your situation is important or your church could have a heart attack. Many churches are resistant to getting in shape because they fear they might die on the treadmill of rapid change. Go slow. Be patient. Be consistent and persistent. Love your congregation and rely on God for your strength.

TIME FRAME

Is there a clear time frame for transition from traditional to contemporary? I don't think the issue revolves around musical style. The issue is church health. The goal of today's church is not to be contemporary or traditional, but healthy and effective in serving people in the name of Christ. It's a tough issue. In a venue situation, there is no transition, which is why I like that solution best. In a blended situation, which is how Saddleback used to be, you are in a state of constant transition looking for the best blends. In any other situation, you are faced with abrupt change.

There is tsunami of change going on in the world of ministry and in culture. Everything around us is changing quickly. We must be wise in how we handle the waves. I don't have a simple right answer, but I know that when a tsunami is coming the wrong thing to do is just stand on the beach and watch.

MY PASTOR ASKED THAT I CHANGE SOMETHING IN HOW I LEAD WORSHIP. WHAT SHOULD I DO?

Worship presentation is subjective and creative. It must be authentic and fluid, not merely a scripted presentation. Many unexpected things can happen in people's hearts as you are leading worship.

On the personal side, criticism of any kind can be painful and sometimes unwelcome. It is very important to receive criticism in a personal and professional way. If someone says they aren't bothered by criticism, then I would think not enough of their heart is on the line. However, the professional part of you must think with your head and not just your heart. Learning from your critics is a great source of growth.

It is helpful for me to separate my *motivation* for leading worship from the *mechanics* of leading worship. My general goal is to support the senior pastor's leadership, and my ultimate goal is to please Jesus Christ. Part of accomplishing those goals is keeping proper perspective. The senior pastor has been given the authority in the church to lead. As worship leaders, we should honor that authority.

That doesn't prevent you from achieving free worship, which is an attitude of the heart, soul, and mind (MATTHEW 22:37). You can't measure the worship in someone's heart based on their physical expression of worship, but you can tell from the works in their life.

Here's how to achieve free worship:

1. Confess your sin to God (NEHEMIAH 9:2–3).

2. Be obedient (2 CORINTHIANS 5:9–10).

3. Make right your personal relationships (MATTHEW 5:23).

4. Practice personal worship (PHILIPPIANS 4:4–9, ROMANS 6:13, 12:1).

5. Pray (PHILIPPIANS 4:6, 2 THESSALONIANS 1:11).

6. Model worship for the congregation (1 CORINTHIANS 11:1).

7. Teach worship and encourage the congregation to anticipate worship (PSALM 119:48, LEVITICUS 23:21).

8. Be prepared (2 TIMOTHY 4:2).

9. Know that the power is not in the production (JOHN 15:5).

A few years ago, my pastor asked me to start using the guitar while leading worship. That was an adjustment for me. I had to learn the guitar parts as well as the lyrics. I did as he requested. I also discovered that some songs did not work as well when I played the guitar, so I transitioned to a mix of sometimes using the guitar and sometimes not using it. The fact that I used the guitar while leading—even though I didn't use it on every song—met my pastor's goal.

When your pastor asks you to change something, ask yourself questions about that request. Will the change reduce or enhance your effectiveness as a worship leader? It is helpful to consider why your pastor has asked this of you, first by thinking it through yourself and then possibly by asking for clarification.

Basically, though, do what the pastor asks.

It's *All*
About You

It's all about you
All about you
Lord, help me to remember

It's all about you
All about you
Lord, help me to remember
It's all about you

Worthy, O Master!
Yes, our God!
Take the glory
The honor
The power
You created it all

This marvelous life
Now and forever

—Rick Muchow

CONCLUSION

Worship isn't something we do. It's what we are. The complete life of a Christian is worship.

I hope that the Q&As, quotes, scriptures, and songs in this book have helped you grow in your love of the One we worship and in the understanding of how worship can be more deeply meaningful throughout your life.

This book isn't comprehensive—it can't be, because worship deserves a lifetime to study—but it's a solid foundation for a richer experience. If it has increased your desire to study worship, please try some of the resources I've recommended. Or if you like, email your questions to me through www.encouragingmusic.com.

May your life of worship grow ever more beautiful in the love, devotion, and passion of the Lord.

Good
AND Worthy
OF *Praise*

You are good and worthy of praise
You are good and worthy of praise
You are beautiful, honorable
True and right and pure
Lord, you're good and worthy
Yes, you are good and worthy of praise

You're the reason that I sing
You're the reason that I'm living

—Rick Muchow

ADDITIONAL RESOURCES

A.W. Tozer, *The Tozer CD-ROM Library* (Cross Country Software: Niagara Falls, New York)

Buddy Owens, *The Way of a Worshipper* (Purpose-Driven Publishing: Lake Forest, CA, 2002)

Charles C. Ryrie, *Basic Theology* (Moody Press: Chicago, 1986, 1999)

Dan Kimbal, *Emerging Worship* (Zondervan: Grand Rapids, Michigan, 2004)

David Jeremiah, *My Heart's Desire* (Turning Point: San Diego, California, 2002)

Jack Hayford, *Worship* (Explaining Worship) (Sovereign World Ltd.: Kent, England, 1996, 2003)

James Strong, LL.D, S.T.D., *Strong's Exhaustive Concordance of the Bible* (Thomas Nelson Publishers: Nashville, 1990)

Joseph L. Garlington, *Worship: The Pattern of Things in Heaven* (Destiny Image Publishers: Shippensburg, PA, 1997)

Louie Giglio, *The Air I Breathe* (Multnomah Publishers: Bend Oregon, 2003)

Matt Redman (and friends), *Inside Out Worship* (Regal Books: Ventura, California, 2005)

Matt Redman, *Facedown* (Regal Books: Ventura, California, 2004

Norman Geisler, *Systematic Theology Volume One* (Bethany House: Minneapolis, Minnesota, 2002)

Patrick Kavanaugh, *Worship a Way of Life* (Chosen Books: Grand Rapids, Michigan, 2001)

Rick Warren, *The Purpose-Driven Church* (Zondervan: Grand Rapids, Michigan, 1995)

Rick Warren, *The Purpose-Driven Life* (Zondervan: Grand Rapids, Michigan, 2002)

Sally Morgenthaler, *Worship Evangelism* (Zondervan: Grand Rapids, Michigan, 1995)

Tom Holladay and Kay Warren, *Foundations* (Zondervan: Grand Rapids, Michigan, 2003)

Wayne Grudem, B*ible Doctrine: Essential Teachings of the Christian Faith* (Zondervan: Grand Rapids, Michigan, 1999)

WordSearch Bible software (Austin, Texas)

The Worship Ring (www.bobsiemon.com/theworshipring)

ACKNOWLEDGEMENTS

Special thanks to Rick and Kay Warren, Jon Walker, Mark Kelly, Scott Schuford, Jeff Brazil, Saddleback Church, The Saddleback Church Creative Arts and Tech Teams, Rob Venneri, Kathy King , Bucky Rosenbaum, Bob Siemon, Jack and Marsha Countryman, Kathy Baker, Troy Johnson and J. Countryman, Purpose Driven, Linda Kimble, Don Buck, Debby Rettino, Kirk DouPonce, Cheryl Venneri, Becky Berg, Tom Brooks, Buddy Owens, Bob Siemon Designs, Dan Cathy, Tom Holladay, Tom Tomasello, Dr. Thurmond George, Dave Fulbright, Sheldon Russell, Don Fugate, Mike McGuffee, Dave Auda, Ron Pratt, George King, Stan Endicott, Chuck Fromm, Morris Chapman, my parents, my inlaws, my extremely supportive and truly beautiful wife Laura Muchow, my five very incredible children: Brandon, Logan, Jordan, Megan, and Nolan . . . and most of all I'd like to thank my Lord and Savior, Jesus Christ, and the God who created me to worship.

ABOUT THE AUTHOR

RICK MUCHOW is worship leader at Saddleback Church, a congregation started by Rick Warren that grew from seven members in 1980 to an average weekly attendance of more than 20,000. Rick Muchow was responsible for developing a Magnification Ministry that is larger than most churches (with more than 1,000 people involved). Now he leads worship at Saddleback and travels with Pastor Rick to lead worship at conferences throughout the world.. He also helps develop worship tools for churches. These tools are available at www.purposedriven.com and www.encouragingmusic.com. Rick has released ten CDs, and more than eighty of his songs are being used in worship throughout the world. He has been featured in numerous music and ministry magazines, and he serves as a teacher and advisor on worship for the over 150,000 church leaders who have attended Purpose-Driven® Church Conferences. Rick and his wife, Laura, are the parents of five children.

One thing I ask of the LORD,

this is what I seek:

that I may dwell in the house of the LORD

all the days of my life,

to gaze upon the beauty of the LORD

and to seek him in his temple.

PSALM 27:4